Praise for *Put Your Intuition to Work:*

"Most people agree that intuition is important to business and life success, but have no idea how to develop it. Even people who access their intuition easily have a difficult time explaining how they do it. Finally, there is a book called *Put Your Intuition to Work* that clearly teaches how to access your intuition and logically put it to good use. Read it and share it with those you live and work with. Thank you Lynn."

—Dr. Marcia Reynolds, President of Covisioning LLC and author of The Discomfort Zone

"Lynn's newest book is superb! That little voice inside your head talking to you? Lynn understands it! I recommend this book to all my business clients and friends because when you can hear that voice speaking more clearly, great things fall into place!"

— Jon Schallert, President, The Schallert Group, Inc.

"Lynn Robinson is surely on to something. Her advice to tap one's intuition to set success in motion is spot-on. What's more, the book's shared stories both illustrate and inspire readers to use Robinson's smart decision-making method in order to unleash potential and triumph in business and beyond. *Put Your Intuition to Work* is at once engaging and valuable—a bona fide win-win."

—Aline Weiller, CEO/Founder, Wordsmith, LLC

"The most important skill for anyone who wants to succeed today, is how to listen to their own brilliant instincts. Lynn Robinson has written a practical, powerful guide to help you know what you really know and to succeed like never before. If you are smart and ambitious, you are going to want to get off the cookie cutter track and listen to your genius. This book is a wise and grounded companion to do just that."

—Tama Kieves, best-selling author of
Inspired & Unstoppable, www. TamaKieves.com

"As someone who has often relied on intuition to manage my business, I appreciated Ms. Robinson's honest, candid writing—which doubled as personal validation for me. Here, Ms. Robinson gives business people permission to put their intuition to work. In addition to delving into success strategies and ways to thrive in the face of change, she provides a trove of actionable steps that lead the reader toward self-trust, which is quite refreshing, given these times when analytics prevail."

—Marcelle Soviero, Owner,
Brain Child: The Magazine for Thinking Mothers

HOW TO SUPERCHARGE YOUR
INNER WISDOM TO THINK FAST
AND MAKE GREAT DECISIONS

put your
intuition
to work

LYNN A. ROBINSON

CAREER
PRESS
THE CAREER PRESS, INC.
Wayne, NJ

Author's Note: Story sources throughout the book come from interviews with clients unless otherwise noted and are used with permission.

PUT YOUR INTUITION TO WORK
EDITED BY JODI BRANDON
TYPESET BY EILEEN MUNSON
Cover design by Jeff Piasky
Gear icon by StudioIcon/shutterstock
Bulb icon by Vector Icons/shutterstock
Printed in the U.S.A.

To order this title, please call toll-free 1-800-CAREER-1 (NJ and Canada: 201-848-0310) to order using VISA or MasterCard, or for further information on books from Career Press.

The Career Press, Inc.
12 Parish Drive
Wayne, NJ 07470
www.careerpress.com

Library of Congress Cataloging-in-Publication Data

CIP Data Available Upon Request.

| Contents |

| Introduction |

Sometimes an answer appears out of nowhere. You've been poring endlessly over a marketing plan for your new product, immersing yourself in data. Something doesn't feel right about it, but you don't know what it is. In dismay, you push away from your desk and head out for a breath of fresh air by taking a walk around the block. Suddenly, the solution pops into your head, and a whole new campaign emerges fully formed. You know you've got a winner! Where did it come from?

You're about to make a big hire, one that will be crucial to the financial success of your business. Human resources has vetted the candidate. The senior staff has interviewed the guy and liked him. He seems like a perfect fit. All is good, right? Then why can't you seem to pick up the phone to offer him the job? Your gut is telling you something is off. When you decide to investigate further, you find out that the candidate's legal troubles include financial mismanagement. You count your blessings that you didn't hire him. What was the clue that tipped you off?

You're bored at your job. You're not feeling challenged by it any longer. You know it's time for a change. You begin to make forays out into the world of potential new work, doing some information interviews, speaking with a recruiter, talking to former colleagues. One morning you get an e-mail suggesting you come in for an interview for a position at a brand-new startup. It sounds promising and right up your alley. After several meetings with the key people, you're offered the job. That's when doubt sets in. Should you give up your "safe" job and take this new offer? Your instincts say yes. Your spouse and colleagues are warning you away. Whom and what to trust? How do you decide?

Intuition can be a powerful tool for creative ideas, perceptive insight, and quick thinking. It can help you decide whether to go all in on an opportunity or, conversely, to run in the other direction. It's a skill that's needed in today's business climate, now more than ever. You need it when you're overwhelmed with data, facts, and figures. Or, in the other extreme, it's crucial when what you're planning is so new, so leading edge, that there's no real data to peruse. You're on your own with your own gut instincts.

Our business world has been dominated by left-brain thinkers who have placed high value on facts, data, and analytics. It's not that those traits and skills are no longer needed. It's that they're no longer sufficient. The capabilities we'll increasingly need to call on are our right-brain resources: creativity, empathy, joyfulness, quick-thinking, meaning, and personal fulfillment.

Is intuitive right-brain thinking a magical skill that only the gifted few can know or develop? The answer is a resounding no!

ʔ   *Put Your Intuition to Work* is filled with techniques, stories, and ideas to help you learn to access and use this powerful inner wisdom that we all possess. This knowledge will allow you to:

ʔ   Make successful decisions when you don't have all the facts.

ʔ   Be guided by what you feel, as well as by what you think.

ʔ   Identify the primary ways that intuition communicates with you.

ʯ   Grow your trust in using intuition for business
    success.

ʯ   Tap your intuition for guidance in hiring and
    employee retention.

ʯ   Envision, attract, and create the life you were
    meant to live.

ʯ   Find creative solutions to difficult problems.

ʯ   Understand your clients and customers from a
    unique vantage point.

This book is based on *Trust Your Gut: How the Power of Intuition Can Grow Your Business*, a book I wrote more than a decade ago. I'm grateful to Career Press and Michael Pye, for giving that book new life in this current one. You'll find many new interviews and techniques as well as leading research to truly *Put Your Intuition to Work* so it can guide you to an extraordinary life.

Chapter 1 | Why Trust Your Gut?

We all have an inner teacher, an inner guide, an inner voice that speaks very clearly but usually not very loudly. That information can be drowned out by the chatter of the mind and the pressure of day-to-day events. But if we quiet down the mind, we can begin to hear what we're not paying attention to. We can find out what's right for us.

—Dean Ornish MD, author and leading healthcare researcher

Whether you call it a gut feeling, an instinct, a hunch, an inner voice, or simply your intuition, there is guidance available to you every moment of the day. That information can help you make successful decisions, alert you to catastrophes before they arise, provide insight into your relationships, and guide you to your own calling and purpose.

There are many signs that your intuition is communicating to you. In any given situation, you can experience such things as a churning stomach when a decision you're about to make is a bad one. You may hear an inner voice, or have an *a-ha!* thought. It could give you a message through a dream, a chance encounter, or a series of synchronicities.

You've seen intuition mentioned in just about every business book in the past decade. It's in the declaration to "Trust your gut" or "Go with your instincts!" It sounds so easy when you read it. It almost sounds as if there's a magic switch labeled "INSIGHT NOW" that others are able to turn on at a moment's notice and instantly receive wise counsel.

Were you asleep in business class when the professor went over instructions about listening to your intuition? Were you out the day he spoke about the importance of intuition as a decision-making tool? Did you get the answer correct on the quiz when asked the percentage of senior executives who attribute their success to intuition? (Hint: According to a June 2014 *Forbes Magazine* article by Roger Dooley, the nswer is 90 percent.) The sad news is, in all likelihood, intuition wasn't mentioned at all.

Who Are the Gut Trusters?

Here's what business leaders are saying about the importance of intuition.

Howard Schultz, the CEO of Starbucks, was asked in a June 2014 *Inc. Magazine* article what he's learned over the past six years. He responded, "With so many competing voices, I learned to trust my own intuitive sense."

Steve Jobs wrote about his decision-making philosophy in his biography. A 2011 article on ReadWrite.com quotes him saying, "I began to realize that an intuitive understanding and consciousness was more significant than abstract thinking and intellectual logical analysis."

Talk show host, actress, and philanthropist Oprah Winfrey wrote in the August 2011 issue of her *O Magazine*, "Learning to trust your instincts, using your intuitive sense of what's best for you, is paramount for any lasting success. I've trusted the still, small voice of intuition my entire life. And the only time I've made mistakes is when I didn't listen."

Warren Bennis is the bestselling author of 20 books on leadership, change, and management. In an article by Winston Brill, he calls intuition his "inner voice" and says that listening to it and trusting it is one of the most important leadership lessons he has learned.

Clothing designer Donna Karan posits in an October 2013 article in the *Huffington Post* that "One of our greatest gifts is our intuition. It is a sixth sense we all have—we just need to learn to tap into and trust it."

Howard Gardner, professor of cognition and education at Harvard University, believes an intuitive leap can mark a breakthrough. He talks about this in the book *The "G" Quotient* by Kirk Snyder: "When you're entering an area where the unknowns are high, and experience is important, if you don't rely on intuition you're cutting yourself short."

Richard Branson, founder of The Virgin Group, wrote an article for Monitor.co.ug entitled "The Power of Delegation" in which he states, "I research new ideas very thoroughly, asking a lot of people about their experiences and their thoughts. But on many occasions I have followed my intuition; you can't make decisions based on numbers and reports alone. It's important to have the courage to follow through on a project if you truly believe it's worth pursuing. We all have an intuitive sense of what's best—follow it!"

What Is It and Why Is It Important?

Intuition. It's a resource that, if nurtured, can lead to increased sales, profitable investments, creative inventions, successful hires, advantageous negotiations, bigger profits, and increased accuracy in forecasting business trends.

Intuition is a skill we all have. Survey after survey indicates that decision-makers in a wide variety of fields rely on it to make successful decisions and choices. We're born with intuition. Perhaps some of us have the ability to tap into it more easily than others. But, like any skill, the more we practice using it, the better we get at it.

What is this gift of intuition? How do we define it? Here are some ways it's commonly described:

⊦   A tool for quick and ready insight.

⊦   A natural mental faculty.

⊦   A gut feeling.

⊦   A sixth sense.

⊦   An inner knowing.

⊦   An instinct.

⊦   A hunch.

⊦   Wisdom from a higher power.

⊦   A still, quiet inner voice.

Where Does Intuition Come From?

There are two schools of thought about the origins of intuition:

Synthesis of prior knowledge: A blend of logic, experience, and subconscious information that's stored in your mind and recalled when needed.

A higher power: Divine intelligence, a "compass of the soul" that guides, informs, and directs you toward success.

To folks in the first category, intuition is a matter of recognizing patterns or cues that ultimately show you what to do. An intuitive firefighter will tell you he saw a pattern to the blaze that made him issue a command to evacuate the building immediately. Later, if pressed on his decision, he might be able to state that the flames were acting in a strange manner, and that fact, combined with a certain smell and roar from the building, indicated an imminent explosion.

He had correctly ascertained that if he didn't get the occupants and his team out of the structure he would lose lives. With seconds to make a decision he processed complex information based on years of knowledge to make what appeared to others around him to be an instinctual act.

An executive interviewing for a key position dismisses one of the applicants, who later turns out to have lied on her resume. When asked how he knew something was wrong, he simply alluded to a gut feeling. However, when questioned more deeply on what raised a red flag about the applicant, he was able to expand on his response: He noted that the interviewee didn't maintain eye contact when answering several key questions. She had shifted uncomfortably in her chair when asked about her responsibilities in a prior position. He also noticed that her response to a subtler question was a bit overenthusiastic.

Whereas both the firefighter and executive just mentioned might point to intuition as a form of pattern recognition, many people also view intuition as a form of spiritual inner guidance. Mark Fisher writes in his book *The Instant Millionaire*, "Listen to that tiny inner voice sleeping in the depths of your mind and give it more freedom to express itself. The more often you repeat the formula, the more powerful it will become and the more surely it will guide you. This is your intuition, the voice of your soul. The road to your secret power."

Sarah Ban Breathnach, president and CEO of Simple Abundance, Inc., and bestselling author, writes about intuition this way in her book *The Simple Abundance Companion*: "Intuition is the subliminal sense that spirit endowed us with to maneuver safely through the maze of real life."

Katy Wells is one of my clients. She describes receiving this "message from her spirit" version of intuition prior to opening her interior decorating business:

I had prayed to be guided to the right career after my husband died. The inner voice I associate with my intuition kept nudging me towards "hanging out my shingle." I also had recurring dreams about decorating people's homes. Finally, after a series of synchronicities that continued to point me in this direction, I found an ideal storefront to rent as my office and landed two clients, all within the same week. This was seven years ago, and I've had a bustling and thriving business ever since.

So what is intuition? Is it immediate knowledge based on past experience and pattern recognition? Or is it guidance that comes to us from a spiritual source? The consensus is, that despite these differences, both explanations are valid. We're going to explore both types of intuition because whichever one you believe in, you're right!

You Can Learn How to Use and Develop It

We all receive intuitive information. Like any skill, the more you practice it, the more you'll improve. As you continue to develop this talent, you'll find you rely on it more and more. The process will no longer feel laborious. It will simply be a matter of checking in with it ("What's my gut say?") and the answer appearing. You'll recognize those inner nudges pointing you in the direction of success and away from bad decisions.

Practice opens up the information flow of intuitive insights. You'll find that answers come unbidden, popping into your mind, offering up creative solutions, and steering you toward prosperity, toward strong leadership and profitable connections with others, and overall toward a happier outlook. And there's a big bonus: You won't be bogged down in hours of analysis and research anymore.

It really does work like that—which is why one of the best decisions you could make right now is to begin to develop your intuition.

As one of my banking executive clients said recently, "I use my intuition to come up with the right answer and then use my logic and research skills to prove what I already knew."

Think back on the past week. Describe an occasion when you had a hunch about something. How did you receive the information? Did it come as a flash of insight? A gut feeling? An inner knowing? Perhaps you had a dream or heard an inner voice.

Did you follow this hunch or cast it aside?

Did your intuition prove to be accurate?

As you begin to pay attention to the many ways you receive intuition, you'll be rewarded with an *increasing* flow of accurate and reliable insight.

Are You a Gut Truster?

Perhaps you're already a "gut truster" and don't even realize you have this skill or talent. Take this brief quiz to find out. Answer each of the following statements with yes or no.

___ I often act on hunches that turn out to be right.

___ I tune in to how I'm feeling before I make a decision.

___ I've argued against an "obvious" or "logical" decision because I just "knew" it wasn't right.

___ I act on the intuitive intelligence I receive.

___ I frequently have *a-ha!* moments that lead to a creative idea or insight.

___ I pay attention to my first impression of a new person or situation.

___ My intuitive insights help me solve problems at work as well as in my personal life.

___ I check in with my gut before making any new decision.

___ I ask my intuition questions throughout the day in order to discern my next steps.

___ I've had dreams that gave me a creative solution to a difficult problem.

___ Intuition enables me to have insight into other people's behavior that allows me to resolve difficulties more quickly.

Scoring

1 or more yes answers:

Congratulations! You have a very high "IQ" (Intuition Quotient.) Increase your conscious use of it and it will serve you even better.

6 to 10 yes answers:

Begin to pay attention to all the ways you receive intuitive impressions and you'll raise your "IQ" in no time.

3 or fewer yes answers:

Time to get out of your head! There is more to life than logic and rationality. Be willing to experiment with using intuition in low-risk situations. You'll build your "intuition muscles" and be rewarded with quick and ready insight in no time.

Throughout this book, I'll give you tools, information, and intuitive success stories from fellow business people. In fact, I predict that with practice, your intuition will have become an old friend by the time you finish the last chapter—a friend who can be counted on for good advice and guidance.

Put Your Intuition to Work Tip

Think about a time you had a sense of something but couldn't quite explain it. Did you discount the information or choose to see it as important and act on it? Begin to pay attention to the many ways that you receive intuitive information. There's no one *right* way—just the way that's right for you.

Chapter 2 | The Many Ways Your Intuition Communicates

There is something to be said about that gut feeling, when we know our next move. Through all the clutter and noise of our daily lives, there is a deep quiet inside that knows when and how to act. Listen to that voice and don't look back.

—Kathleen Kennedy, American producer and president of Lucasfilm Ltd.

Steve Lishansky, CEO of Optimize International and author of *The Ultimate Sales Revolution,* describes how intuition helped him land his first major corporate client. Though he'd never worked with a company larger than mid-size, his friend Linda had put him in touch with a contact of hers. This is how Steve found himself talking to Tony, who was a key information technology executive at a Fortune 500 company.

However, Steve knew nothing about IT. Plus, the company itself was a financial services company and—you guessed it— Steve had never dealt with financial services, either. It was a daunting task Steve faced, but he knew that if he was going to take advantage of the opportunity in front of him, he needed to make the call to set up a meeting.

"So, Steve," Tony said after a quick handshake and a brief introduction, "I understand you'd be worth talking to about our project. What do you do?" Steve didn't hesitate. He jumped right in with an intuitive flash that set up the whole conversation. "I help companies improve their performance. Rather than bore you with a laundry list of what we do, why don't you explain a few of your specific issues, and I'll tell you what I'd do with them."

Tony raised an eyebrow, then proceeded to discuss his organizational challenges. Steve and Tony started to converse, and as they did Steve began to see questions appear in his mind. He was surprised—but not too surprised. He was, after all, an intuition "believer." So he simply relaxed, followed his intuition, and asked Tony the questions that appeared.

As Tony answered the questions, he became excited. "I never thought of it that way before," he exclaimed. Steve asked more questions and Tony answered them all. At the end of the meeting, Tony told Steve they had worked with another consultant for four frustrating months trying to get him to understand what they were after. "And in just one hour," Tony said, "you not only got it, but I'm really clear about how you can help us!"

Bottom line: Tony introduced Steve to his boss, the CIO, who was similarly impressed, and Steve, with the help of his intuition, had his first Fortune 500 assignment, which turned out to be worth more than a million dollars in the course of this relationship.

Steve says of that day, "It was an absolutely effortless conversation. An insightful line of questioning just kept on appearing, and as Tony came up with answers, he was led to greater and greater clarity. At the end of the conversation, he made an amazing statement. He said 'You know, if my people could do with their clients what you just did with me, we'd have no problems.' I knew at that moment what an extraordinary meeting had just taken place. We ended up producing dramatic, highly valued results with their organization. Tony became a friend, and this company became one of my best clients."

Why Pay Attention to Intuition?

Steve listened to his intuition at a critical moment in his business life. He heard it. He heeded it. And he scored a major contract. But listening to your intuition doesn't always lead directly to the bottom line. Nevertheless, there are plenty of times when it's important to tune in and listen up. For example:

ⴕ   When there's insufficient data.

ⴕ   When you need to make a decision quickly.

ⴕ   When there's too much information.

ⴕ   When the data is conflicting.

ⴕ   When your data seems to support several different options.

ⴕ   When your individual or group vision has become cloudy.

ⴕ   When you're stuck and can't "think" your way out.

ⴕ   When you need to come up with outside-the-box ideas.

How Do You Receive Intuition?

There is no right or wrong way to receive intuitive information. However, you probably have a predominate mode of receiving its wisdom. Here are some common ways intuition communicates.

Physical Sensations

These include a knot in your stomach, hot flash, cold shivers, a tension in your neck or shoulders, or a generalized sense of lightness or heaviness.

Example: My client Edward described a major business decision he had to make. His company had decided to expand their operations and open branch offices in four key cities in the United States. There had been a good deal of money and time invested in research and analysis of which geographical area would be most profitable for their company. Whenever he met with his staff to work on logistical details about the sites for the business expansion, he had what he describes as a "knot in my stomach" about one of the cities. The other three locations that were chosen he felt great about. He gave a "go ahead" to these and said "no" to the city he felt queasy about. A few months later he learned that this city had been devastated by a major hurricane. Needless to say, he was very glad he had chosen to trust that gut feeling.

Emotion

Intuitive information often comes through your emotions. Feelings of relief, enthusiasm, passion, eagerness, and excitement characterize good decisions. Conversely, if you're making a decision that may lead you astray, you'll likely feel heavy, depressed, weighted down, drained, bored, or enervated.

Example: You've been feeling overwhelmed lately and realize you need to examine your lifestyle with an eye to letting go of some activities. As you examine your list of items, which of them do you look at and immediately feel drained? Which things make you feel excited? Those responses are your intuition at work! Move away or let go of the ones that deplete you, and keep the ones that energize you.

Auditory

Many people report a "still, quiet inner voice." It may sound perceptively different from your normal everyday inner chatter. People often characterize it as a non-judgmental or compassionate voice.

Example: My fledging intuitive consulting business began as the result of this type of intuition. I walked into a funeral service for a friend. I heard an inner voice saying "Sit there." My attention was drawn to an empty seat next to one of the few people in the room I didn't know. Always a believer in trusting these auditory messages, I sat next to her. The short version of the story is that my seatmate turned out to be a reporter for the *Boston Globe* newspaper. She wrote a story about my unusual consulting business. As a result, more than 300 people called me to request my services and my new career was born.

Image

The old adage "A picture is worth a thousand words" pertains to this form of intuitive information. Intuition often communicates through symbolic images.

Example: My client Karen was seeking venture capital for her skincare product line. She had presented her business plan at an investors meeting and had the happy outcome of two groups seemingly interested in working with her. They presented equally attractive offers. As she studied her pros and cons list, Karen felt more and more confused about which one to work with.

I asked her to close her eyes, take a deep breath, relax, and envision each of the two offers with the intention of receiving an intuitive response. Within a few moments, she opened her eyes and laughed. She had seen an image of one of the potential investors holding a huge sign that said, "My way!" The insight she received was that this individual was probably rather difficult to work with, only wanting to do things *his* way. Karen perceived through this image that he was not particularly collaborative, an issue that was of utmost importance to her. She later had her symbolic instinct confirmed when talking with another person who had worked with this investor.

Epiphany

Otherwise known as "a-ha" moments, epiphanies are usually a flash of insight or a "knowing." People often report they suddenly know something but don't know where the insight came from. Epiphanies frequently arrive when you least expect them—while showering, washing the dishes, walking the dog, whenever.

Example: Thomas Edison, one of the most prolific inventors of all time, was a great believer in intuition. He registered a new patent an average of every two weeks of his adult life. He carried a 200-page notebook with him at all times to record flashes of inspiration. As one biographer described it, Edison would be talking with friends or eating, "when something he saw, a topic of conversation, or an intruding memory, jogged up a technological possibility." At the time of his death, Edison had filled 3,400 such notebooks.

Dreams

Dreams can provide a rich source of guidance for insight in all forms when you learn how to use them. Painter Vincent van Gogh once said, "I dream my painting, and then I paint my dream." People report coming up with creative solutions, answers to complex issues, moneymaking ideas, and inventions—all while sound asleep.

Example: When I had the experience of meeting the *Boston Globe* reporter, I was still working as an operations manager for a software company. The experience of gaining more than 300 clients virtually overnight might be some people's idea of a dream come true. To me it was anxiety-producing. I was fearful of giving up my "normal" job, with benefits and a weekly paycheck, to be out on my own as a consultant. "Could I keep both jobs?" was the question I asked myself as I drifted off to sleep. When I awakened in the morning, I had to laugh. In my dream, I was out on a lake in canoes. Yes, plural! I had one foot in one canoe and the other foot in another canoe, and they were headed in opposite directions! I took that as a very clear sign that I wasn't meant to begin my consulting business while holding on to my day job. I gave my notice that day and never looked back.

Should You Use Proven Data or Intuition?

The answer is both! Rosa Harris wrote a February 2015 Fortune.com article entitled "Only Human: The Emotional Logic of Business Decisions" in which she stated, "Data. It is a powerful tool for executives, delivering them greater analytical depth than ever before. What does this mean for the decision-making process? Are executives leaning deeper into the numbers to help make important choices? Undoubtedly, the answer is yes, but despite vast pools of information, the intuitive still precedes the rational when it comes to business decisions." It was the key finding derived from an expansive research study conducted by the FORTUNE Knowledge Group in collaboration with Gyro, a global advertising agency:

> The Gyro.com study polled 720 senior executives (88% of whom had director-level titles or higher) in June 2014 to explore how emotions and other subjective factors influence business decision-making. Among the findings, results show that executives increasingly rely on emotions, intuition, or "gut feelings" when making important choices. Our respondents strongly agree that as the amount of information available to them increases—often to the point of becoming overwhelming—they place greater emphasis on "softer" factors, such as a business partner's corporate culture and reputation.

We've all had those intuitive moments when faced with a choice at work or in your personal life. However they come to you, pay attention. You might be contemplating a potential deal with a new client at work. All signs point to a successful outcome, and yet you can't seem to shake the feeling that something is "off" or wrong. You're likely to dismiss this feeling as illogical or irrational. However, after signing the contract and working with the client, you discover your intuition was right all along. Why didn't you pay attention?

We use our intuition all the time for all sorts of decisions. It's an incredibly important skill. Although it's difficult to explain *where* the information comes from, it's possible to encourage and develop it. Doing so will help you supercharge your inner wisdom so that you can think fast and make great decisions.

If using intuition is new to you, keep reading! You'll find a wealth of information on these pages to get you started. If you're an old hand at intuition and you've been listening to it for years, you, too, can expect to find new techniques, ideas, and processes that will deepen your connection to this wellspring of knowledge.

Put Your Intuition to Work Tip
Intuitive information primarily communicates through feelings, images, dreams, aha moments, an inner voice and physical sensations. Begin to pay attention to how *your* intuition communicates with you. As you do, you'll be rewarded with faster and more accurate insight.

||| Put Your Intuition to Work Technique |||
Cultivate "A-ha" Moments

*Intuition is the key to everything, in painting, filmmaking, business—
everything. I think you could have an intellectual ability, but if you can
sharpen your intuition, which they say is emotion and intellect joining
together, then a knowingness occurs.*

—David Lynch, director

It's the curse of anyone trying to trust their intuition: nothing comes, no answers, nada. And then—voila!—the "a-ha" moment. An idea you previously hadn't considered simply pops into your mind. These seem to come when you least expect them and usually not when you're engaged in serious and solemn thought.

What can you do to invite this kind of intuitive message? Get clear about what you want and be open to the guidance.

Step 1: What do you want?

Here's a list of examples. I want a winning idea for:

The theme for our annual meeting.

My next direct mail piece.

Our new ad campaign.

Approaching the acquisition committee.

Boosting sales at our winter conference.

Step 2: Chill out!

What do you enjoy that's creative and relatively mindless? Do it. For some it's knitting, for others it might be completing a crossword puzzle, cooking, or playing a musical instrument. You want to create a period of downtime where you're simply enjoying yourself and not thinking about your problem or concern. Be advised that the "a-ha" message may not pop into your mind during this creative interval, but it may happen when you least expect it at some point during the day.

Step 3: Listen

Intuitive insights have a distinct feel. Remember the ad campaign for V-8 juice? The actors had little thought balloons that said, "I could have had a V-8!" "A-ha" moments are just like that. People often describe them as a "pop" of inspiration or ideas. You can't force them to happen. You create an environment that allows them to occur. Just like that, a wonderful idea will come to you.

Chapter 3 | Uncover Your Hidden Intelligence

Intuition is data. It's just that human intuition is processed in the ultimate black box algorithm—the human brain—and none of us own the IP on that (at least not yet).

—Joshua Reynolds, columnist for MarketingLand

Sharon is the chief operating officer for a rapidly growing national technology company. She says:

I use intuition all the time. I'm not sure how people survive without it in a fast-paced industry like high tech. I'm constantly in the position of having to make quick decisions when I don't have all the facts. I would love to have the luxury of taking days or even weeks to make crucial decisions. That's just not possible.

For me, intuition comes in two forms. One, I believe, is made up of the knowledge that I have in this field. When I need to make a quick decision, I tap a lot of subsconscious information that rises to the surface and enables me to sift through data swiftly and accurately.

My technique is to gather as much data as I can and take some time to simply read it and sit with it. Often the information is contradictory. My research department suggests one thing, sales staff may be indicating yet another direction. I take it all in and then I close my eyes and ask myself questions: "If I make this choice, will it be successful?" Or "Is this the right direction?". I just let myself emotionally feel the answers. The information arrives in a way that I can only describe as a "knowing." When an answer is the intuitive right one, there's an odd combination of it feeling correct along with a sense of openness and relief. The wrong answer I experience as tension and heaviness. In addition, I may also hear something like the sound on a game show when the contestant offers the wrong answer!

The second way intuition communicates is through Divine guidance. I'm not a religious person but I have a strong spiritual belief system. This form of intuition comes to me more frequently with people—my staff, my clients, friends, and my family.

In this case, I more often hear the information I need. For example, I recently was having a rather heated conversation with a member of my executive team. We both had strong feelings about the rightness of our respective positions. I have to admit that I'm an experienced debater and will confess that I like to win arguments. This has not always worked to my benefit improving business comunication!

In this conversation I actually heard the words "Sharon, let this go. Sleep on it and meet again tomorrow." Now, my logical mind did not want to do this! However, I've learned to heed these messages. I did as I was told, suggesting to my team member a time to continue the conversation the next morning. When I woke up, darn it, I realized that my team member had a strong point and was probably right. I was able to pick up our conversation the next day, and we resolved things quickly and amicably. When I listen to and act on these auditory intuitions, things work out so much better!

The interesting thing about these auditory messages is that they're often quite short yet seem packed with information. I frequently meet with the founder of my company. He's a very demanding guy who expects immediate answers and results. Fortunately, he's learned to respect my intuition.

During a conversation a few weeks ago, he was insisting we make a change to how we were marketing a certain product. My auditory message lit up with the answer "Wait on this." I told him I'd look into the situation further and get back to him with a solution in two weeks.

Right around that time, a competitor came out with a similar product that turned out to have a lot of problems. They had to temporarily withdraw it from the market. It made our product look golden in comparison. We gained a lot of positive publicity and no new marketing direction was needed. Heeding that inner voice has helped me with so many varied decisions!

Like Sharon, we've all had experiences where our logic tells us one thing and our intuition says another. Some business veterans who have made bad choices and gone against their gut instincts refer to these as the "woulda coulda shoulda" experience. If I would have trusted my intuition, I could have done well and this better thing should have happened.

Good Choice/Bad Choice Quiz

To help you determine whether a choice you're making is the best direction to follow, try this. Write several sentences on a notepad about a decision you're about to make. For the purpose of this exercise, give yourself two options: choice A or choice B.

Imagine yourself making the decision to go with choice A. Close your eyes and ask yourself the following questions. Then repeat the exercise with choice B.

How do you feel about this decision?

A: Up. Enthusiastic.

B: Down. Depressed.

How do you physically experience this decision?

A: Lightness, openness, flexibility.

B: Stomach or shoulders tighten at the thought of pursuing this choice.

Do you receive any visual impressions when thinking about this choice?

A: Positive images surround the symbolic representation of this decision.

B: I see an X through the decision, or I see some other negative image.

Of course these are just illustrations of the many ways intuition might speak to you on whether you're about to make a good choice or a bad one. Part of learning to develop your intuition is becoming familiar with the ways in which it communicates to you. You have your own personalized way you receive the information.

In fact, it's much like learning a foreign language. At first it may be unfamiliar to you, yet, with practice, you begin to notice subtle nuances, shades, and characteristics that allow you to recognize the intuitive messages.

Here's another way to see if you're on the right track with a decision you're about to make. Take the following quick quiz to see how your intuition measures up.

The One-Minute Intuition Checklist

⊦ Think of a problem or challenge you're facing. Write a few paragraphs about it in a journal or your computer.

⊦ Now think of one possible course of action. Summarize it into a sentence. "My decision is _____."

⊦ Hold that decision in your mind as you go through the following checklist, answering yes or no to each question.

_____Do you feel excited or energized by this decision?

_____Do you feel open to making this change?

_____You know you have other choices, but does this one feel right?

_____Is this the right time to act on this decision?

_____Does this decision feel right in your gut?

_____Can you see the successful completion of this decision?

_____Close your eyes and think of an image that represents this decision. Did you receive a positive image?

Your One-Minute Intuition Analysis

If you answered yes to all seven questions: Your intuition is giving you a clear go-ahead. It's time to take action!

If you answered no to one question: Try to modiify your decision and see if it affects your score in a positive direction.

If you answered no to two questions: Perhaps your decision required a leap of faith that was a little too big. Are there some smaller steps you could take?

If you answered no to three questions: Timing is always important in decision-making. If you didn't receive a resounding *yes!* from your intuition, it may not be the right time for you to make a change.

If you answered no to four questions: It's normal to feel at least a little anxious when something changes in our lives. Is there part of the decision you could adjust that would make you more comfortable?

If you answered no to five or more questions: Stop! Your intuition is telling you this is clearly not a good decision for you.

Intuition Doesn't Always Tell You *Why*

The problematic part of using intuition is that often you don't know why you're being guided toward or away from something until after the fact. A client, Jake, related a story about his plan to buy a second home in California. He knew it was an area that was experiencing a big real estate boom and he wanted to buy while he could still afford the kind of home he and his wife wanted. They worked with a real estate broker and identified the perfect house. It was in a community they liked. It was a short walk to the beach, and some close friends lived nearby.

Everything was perfect except Jake found he kept putting off the decision to say yes and move ahead on the deal. He says:

I'm not usually a procrastinator. I think of myself as a decisive person. Besides that, I had run all the numbers. Everything checked out. It appeared to be a slam-dunk decision.

This was becoming a somewhat serious issue between my wife and me. But I couldn't shake the feeling that this wasn't a good decision. I just couldn't figure out why! It was driving me crazy. Fortunately the decision was taken out of my hands when the broker called and told us the sellers were going to accept an offer from another party.

Several months later, Jake was watching the news. The reporter was describing how the fires were engulfing the community they'd been interested in. High winds were fanning the flames and many of the expensive homes were being destroyed. Camera crews captured a scene of firefighters working to douse flames on a familiar-looking place. "Suddenly," Jake says, "I realized this was 'our' house I was looking at and then it all made sense. I felt awful for the people who owned the place. It could easily have been us. But I also felt thankful I had trusted my gut."

Jake's choice was an almost purely intuitive one. However, making a successful decision is usually a combination of the rational/analytical and the intuitive. Sometimes it's difficult to differentiate the two! Following are a few more ideas to consider when making a decision.

Don't discount your gut feelings. Combine your critical-thinking abilities with your instincts. Are there other clues your body is giving you about a decision? Tight shoulders, cold hands, and a headache are commonly noted signals that something is "off."

If appropriate to the decision, pay attention to nonverbal cues of the people involved, such as body language and facial expressions. They're apt to give you additional insight.

Be wary of relying completely on feelings and emotions when making decisions. Many of the people interviewed for this book noted that they had an "intuitive hit" or idea, but felt most comfortable backing up that inner wisdom with further research, discussion or study. As Apple Computer's Tim Cook stated in a 2010 commencement speech at Auburn University, "For the most important decisions in your life, trust your intuition, and then work with everything you have to prove it right.

It's a bit difficult to not be swayed by strong feelings and emotions when making a decision. In the next chapter, I'll talk about the importance of your self-talk and its relevance to receiving intuitive guidance.

Put Your Intuition to Work Tip
Intuition is like learning a foreign language. At first it may be unfamiliar to you, yet, with practice, you begin to notice subtle nuances, shades, and characteristics that allow you to recognize the intuitive messages.

Chapter 4 | Open Your Mind to New Ideas

Since your conscious mind can hold only one thought at a time, either positive or negative, if you deliberately choose a positive thought to dwell upon, you keep your mind optimistic and your emotions positive. Since your thoughts and feelings determine your actions, you will tend to be a more constructive person and you will move much more rapidly toward the goals that you have chosen.

— Brian Tracy, author and speaker

John had felt optimistic and hopeful earlier in the year when he left the advertising agency he was working for in order to start his own graphic design firm. However, on this particular morning, he was sitting at his desk beleaguered by a sense of failure. He had a headache. His phone hadn't rung all day. If you could have heard the thoughts going through John's mind, you would have discovered he had a very pessimistic focus. Listen in...

Why aren't any of these new business initiatives working?

Am I in the wrong business?

Why is Sue having luck with her new business and I'm not?

Have I come into this business at precisely the wrong time?

Why am I having endless problems with my subcontractors?

Will I ever make serious money?

Maybe I'm not cut out for being self-employed.

What am I doing wrong?

Have you ever tried talking with a friend who was stuck in a negative thinking pattern similar to John's? If so, you may have offered one constructive suggestion after another and received little or no response. Your friend was basically not open to your contribution.

Intuition operates in much the same way. If your mind is closed to new ideas, there's simply no room for inspired input from your eager-to-help inner consultant.

When John began to recognize that his unhelpful mental state wasn't producing the answers he needed, he began to shift his focus. He said he remembers something I had said in one of our consulting sessions: "The quality of the questions you ask yourself will determine the quality of the answers you get back." He realized he wasn't asking very good questions!

Learn to Shift Your Focus

Edward de Bono, a leading authority on creativity thinking, is quoted on the BrainyQuotes.com Website as saying, "Sometimes the situation is only a problem because it is looked at in a certain way. Looked at in another way, the right course of action may be so obvious that the problem no longer exists."

John realized that all of his concerns were focused on the theme of "What am I doing wrong?" His whole internal concentration was on **what's wrong**. In de Bono's way of thinking, John was asking the wrong question. He decided to grab his laptop and sit outside in the early summer sun. Listening to the birds sing put him into a slightly better mood. He began to write about what he wanted to create in his business.

I want to create:

> *Customers I enjoy working with who refer me to other great clients.*

> *A monthly net income of at least $10,000.*

> *An easy and enjoyable lifestyle that allows time for me to attend my kids' after-school and weekend events.*

> *A great team of subcontractors who I can count on to deliver an excellent product or service.*

> *Positive press for my graphic design business.*

As John continued his list, he found himself in an even better frame of mind. His thinking was clearer. He felt open to new possibilities. Ideas began to pop into his head.

As he sat outside basking in the sun, he began to shift his focus to questions such as "How can I increase my visibility?" and "What can I do to attract my favorite type of clients?" and "How could I make all this easier?" He discovered that when he was more open-minded and less down on himself and his efforts, the answers that would lead him to success began to come to him more easily.

By the end of his self-imposed break, he had come up with some creative marketing ideas as well as a new approach to provide incentives to current clients who introduced him to new ones. Best of all, when he got back to his office, he found that a potential new client had called with an interesting design project.

What Do You Want to Create?

Sally had a slightly different situation. She'd been out of work for four months and was feeling a little desperate to be back and involved in her career as a CIO in the banking industry. A single mother with a 14-year-old daughter, her last position ended when her former bank was merged with a larger one. She was networking with everyone she knew and had been on several job interviews that sounded promising. But so far, no firm offers.

Sally was a type-A personality in the best of circumstances and she was finding the lack of structure in her newly jobless life a bit overwhelming. She tried to fill up each day with endless to-do lists and appointments that kept her mind and body occupied.

At the end of one Friday afternoon, she collapsed on her sofa in tears. Her ex-husband had picked up their daughter and she faced a weekend by herself. A flood of worries encompassed her: *What if I don't find another CIO job? Maybe I should be thinking of another type of position. What if I don't have what it takes? What if I get an offer in another area of the country? How will that affect my daughter?* The more she thought about her life and career in that way, the more upset she got.

At the end of an hour of frantic worrying, she uncharacteristically fell asleep. She awoke at around eight o'clock and made some dinner. She realized she felt a little calmer. One question seemed to keep forming in her mind: *What can I do to be at peace?*

That was a very different kind of question for Sally to ask herself. Always frantic and on the go at both her former job and at home, she'd never really stopped to consider the idea of being at peace. It was a totally foreign notion. Simply asking the question made her feel calmer and slightly more optimistic.

She sat down with her reheated takeout food, left over from the previous night's dinner, and felt open to a new direction. The fear she had felt washed away, and suddenly the world seemed full of possibilities.

The Power of a Good Question

Bestselling author Brian Tracy wrote on his blog, "How to Trigger Great Decisions": "A major stimulant to creative thinking is focused questions. There is something about a well-worded question that often penetrates to the heart of the matter and triggers new ideas and insights."

What are examples of the focused questions that Tracy refers to? Think about some of the concerns and challenges you face today in your business or at your office. Instead of worrying about them, form them into a question that will evoke intuitive answers. In order to do this most effectively, it's best to avoid questions that would suggest a yes or no answer.

If you ask yourself open-ended questions like "How can I...?" and "What can be done to...?" you're allowing answers that will add insight and lead you to success.

Here are some examples:

ǂ How can I better understand the needs of my customers?

ǂ What can be done to improve the quality of our service?

ǂ How can we improve employee retention and productivity?

ǂ What do I need to know about this upcoming client meeting?

Ray was feeling very frustrated that his products and services for financial companies were not selling as quickly as he knew they should. He had trusted his intuition *and* his considerable business acumen to start his enterprise, and had been successful at getting in front of decision-makers for many Fortune 500 companies. The sales cycle from start to finish was simply taking too long and was costing him money.

Ray said he sat down at the couch in his office, closed his eyes, centered himself, took a deep breath, exhaled slowly, and asked simply, "What could we do to improve sales?" He laughed:

I wish I could say a big, booming voice from above gave me the answer! But honestly, that would have scared me half to death! Instead, I saw an image of a menu. At the top it said, "A la carte." As I sat there it occurred to me that perhaps we were trying to sell a product that had too many features. Dividing the product into smaller portions made it easier to understand and wouldn't overwhelm the buyer. We implemented this idea and sales turned around dramatically within the month.

Ray's experience makes a case for the fact that intuitive answers come most easily when you're in a calm and relaxed state of mind. You don't need to take a long break. Simply put your calls on hold, shut the door, close your eyes, and ask your questions!

How to Stay Open to Intuitive Ideas

What are some other ways to stay positive and open to intuitive information? Here are four ideas:

Get Clear About Your Ideal Outcome

Understand that it's human nature to go through ups and downs. When you're having a tough time, take a step back. Look at the situation that's causing your concern. Take a deep breath. Ask yourself what you want to accomplish. Once you have that clarity, ask yourself, "What could I do right now, in this moment, to proceed with more confidence?

Pay Aattention to Any Unconstructive Thoughts

What were you saying to yourself preceding your negative emotional state? You'll likely discover that there was a series of unhelpful or inaccurate statements you were making to yourself. What do you want to say to yourself instead? Choose general phrases such as "I'll figure out this out and get moving in the right direction again." Or "This feels bad right now, but I have some good strategies that I know will work." Or "I know there's a perfect solution to this situation and my intuition is guiding me to it."

Crises Tend to Be Self-Limiting

Remind yourself that your situation is only temporary. We all have inevitable setbacks. Practice observing your thoughts and emotions with compassion. See the issue before you as a single event. Resist the impulse to be a catastrophist and imagine doom and gloom in your future. Don't overwhelm yourself with possible "what if this happens?!" scenarios. When the going gets tough, the "one step at a time" strategy often works best.

Take Inspired Action

When we're upset about something, we tend to ruminate on it. You go over the same thing again and again and usually feel worse as you get into a rut in your thinking. You think you're going to get insight, but you're really just rehashing the events or circumstances. Ask yourself, "What could I do right now to feel better about this?" Answers might include to get more information, to talk to someone who's involved in the issue, or to make a choice to come back to your concerns after a walk.

Finally, keep your thoughts on your goals, intentions, hopes and dreams. When you can do this, intuitive information will come forth that will direct you in the fastest and easiest way to get there. What's currently good about your life and work? What are you grateful for? Staying positive and optimistic opens the flow of the information.

Put Your Intuition to Work Tip
Keep your self-talk positive. Use your imagination to visualize your goals and dreams. Ask for intuitive guidance. Listen to it. Take action on what you receive. There's nothing that can stop you from being the success you're meant to be.

| | | Put Your Intuition to Work Technique | | |
The Magic of Metaphor

The greatest thing by far is to be a master of metaphor. It is the one thing that cannot be learned from others; and it is also a sign of genius, since a good metaphor implies intuitive perception of the similarity in dissimilars.

—Aristotle

The use of metaphors is a wonderful way to unleash your creative muse. A metaphor is simply a different way of thinking about something. Using metaphor to compare your situation to something else is one of the easiest techniques to get ideas flowing.

Roger Von Oech wrote one of the classic books on creativity, entitled *A Whack on the Side of the Head*, in which he states, "There is always a connection between the random thing you select and your problem—and your job is to find it. We humans are quite good at finding patterns and meaning in the world around us—even if none were intended. Whatever you find will add insight into your problem."

Step 1: Define the problem. Frame the problem as a question. For example, consumer focus groups have revealed that your product doesn't have sufficient brand recognition. Your question becomes "How can we increase brand recognition?"

Step 2: Define your key concept. Start with the most basic idea for your product. What is it that you most want your customer or buyer to know? This might be "healthy" or "cost effective" or "innovative" or "ideal for baby boomers."

Step 3: Create a symbolic representation of your key concept. You can use words or visuals. Try crayons, paint, or colored pens. Rip pictures out of magazines if that helps get your creative juices flowing! Draw, write, or paste images that reflect the best metaphor of the benefit you want to communicate.

Step 4: Use sentence completion. Remember Tom Hanks's famous line in the movie *Forrest Gump*? "Life is like a box of chocolates." Similes are a comparison between two objects using the words *like* or *as*. A simile can help you find a metaphor.

This brand, service, or product is like _____.

The benefit to the consumer of this brand, product, or service is like _____.

A metaphor can be used to characterize the personality of the brand. A branding campaign for a healthy fast food company uses the visual metaphor of a runner, for example, to characterize the company's product as quick and healthy.

Step 5: Choose a random object or action. To generate some creative ideas, compare your product or service to an arbitrary object or a situation. For example, how is your brand similar to:

Running a race?	Downhill skiing?
Doing stand-up comedy?	Being a new parent of twins?
Being a politician?	An internet dating service?
Political office?	Being a motivational speaker?

Step 6: Reflect and choose. What have you come up with so far? Are there images, feelings, or concepts that have grabbed you? That's your intuition speaking. It informs you of the best ideas based on all your creative input. Now do what Nike suggests in their ad campaigns: Just do it!

Chapter 5 | Time for a Gut Check

Trusting your gut. Using your 6th Sense. Having a hunch. These are all ways of describing your built-in intuition or guidance system. We all have it. In fact, your gut makes more neuro-chemicals than your brain. Some of you may feel you have lost your gut-brain, but there are many ways to get it back. Simply desiring to develop your intuition—or regain it—is a good start.
—Christiane Northrup, MD, author and women's health expert

Allen had a decision to make. He sat in my office looking extremely distressed for a man who had two equally enticing job offers. He had spent a sleepless night going over his pros and cons list in a desperate attempt to make the right choice. It was an important career decision for him and he didn't want to make the wrong move.

Company A offered him a significant increase in salary and benefits, an opportunity to make a difference as a leader in his field, and a geographic move that both he and his family found appealing.

Company B had been around longer, had a good reputation in this industry, and seemed to offer the potential for more stability. They were offering an opportunity for investment in the company that could really pay off for Allen in the long run.

We discussed the offers at length, along with Allen's impressions of the companies and the people he interviewed with. The more we discussed the facts of the two positions, the more agitated he became. He was leaning toward accepting the offer from Company B largely because stability was important to his family and him, and he felt that corporation presented the best opportunity.

Something still didn't feel right, so I suggested he do something a little out of the ordinary for him: close his eyes, take a deep breath, and relax. I asked him to sit quietly for a few moments, and put all the logic and facts out of his mind as best he could and simply focus on the in and out of his breath.

When he appeared to be settled, I said in a quiet voice, "Imagine that you're taking the job with Company A. Pay attention to any feelings, images, knowings, or body sensations you have as you contemplate this decision." I waited about 30 seconds. "Next," I said, "imagine you're taking the job with Company B."

I was prepared to wait for him to process this and he surprised me by exclaiming "Oh!" and opening his eyes. What happened? He explained that as I spoke the words *Company B* he had an immediate image of the company logo with a huge X through it accompanied by a sinking feeling and a queasiness in his belly.

He instantly tried to come up with some logical reasons for this response. I explained that in conducting this brief exercise, we were asking for intuitive information that might assist him with his decision. This inner guidance will provide information that we may not consciously be aware of.

The imagery and feeling seemed fairly obvious to me. An X through the logo would appear to indicate "don't go there," or at the very least that there was something wrong. The sinking feeling was also an important clue. If a decision lacks energy or vitality, it's your intuition trying to steer you away from that choice or situation. Though I wasn't suggesting Allen make a decision based entirely on this insight, he should add it to the mix of information he already had.

Allen left my office promising to call me to tell me the results of his decision-making. I didn't hear from him again until several months had passed. He was light-hearted and laughing on the phone. He explained that after again examining his pros and cons list *and* listening to his intuition he had taken the job with Company A. He described it as a real struggle because he truly wanted the stability of the other company.

Here's where the story takes an interesting turn: Allen had just learned that Company B had unexpectedly filed for bankruptcy. When he heard this, he suddenly understood the information his intuition had provided. It all made sense. He was happy he had listened.

The "Brain" in Your Belly

Have you ever had a knot in your stomach? It's a commonly accepted indicator that something is amiss. You're stressed about a decision. It's a warning of sorts.

Perhaps you're about to hire the wrong person or take your team into perilous territory. The tension in your belly is part of your intuitive physical system communicating "Danger ahead. Redirection is needed!"

Many scientists believe we have two brains: the one between our ears, and the lesser known, but equally important one in our gut. They communicate with each other. When your head gets upset, your stomach takes notice—and vise versa.

The next time you're faced with a decision, large or small, check in with your gut. Does an option you're considering feel *off* or *right* in your belly?

Is your stomach tied in knots at the thought of making an offer to the person you just interviewed, or does it feel relaxed and at ease?

Here are some questions to ask:

Is there an alternative that feels better?

Is this the right time to make this decision? Does waiting a few hours (or days, weeks, or months) feel better?

Do you need more information before making this decision?

Does the whole thing feel wrong? Or just part of it?

What would make this decision feel right?

Is there a question or issue that keeps coming to mind that you've been dismissing? Pay attention to it. Bring it to your conscious awareness and check in with your gut. It may provide some valuable information about the correct course of action.

Intuition is a skill that, when practiced, can be honed to perfection. Imagine having a reliable "gut check" meter you can use each time you need to make a decision! As you've been reading this book, you may have begun to recognize the primary way you receive intuitive messages.

It's More Than Your Gut

The term *gut feeling* is often used generically for a whole host of other body sensations. Physical sensations are a huge part of our intuitive guidance system. When I asked people to describe their "gut" feeling in more detail, I received a surprising variety of answers, including:

- A vibration through my whole body.
- A mild electric zing.
- Chills up and down my spine.
- A warm surge of energy though my body.
- A buzzing around my head.
- "Goosebumps" on my arms.
- My left knee hurts.
- My stomach knots up.
- Indigestion.

⊦ Generalized tension in my body that wasn't there previously.

⊦ I get cold feet.

There were many more answers, but suffice to say, the body's owner was aware when they were receiving an intuitive communication.

One entrepreneur I spoke with said she was contemplating taking on a new piece of business. However, whenever she picked up the phone to dial the prospective client to say yes, she felt like "someone pulled the plug on my energy." She ended up turning the client down. Later she overheard someone at a networking event talking about this client and describing how incredibly difficult they were to work with. "It was like my mind was telling me to go ahead. But my body was smarter," she said.

Pay Attention to the Physical Cues

So, how do you learn to interpret these physical messages? First, simply be aware of what's going on with your own body. Think back to a successful decision you've made over the past few days How did it feel in your body? Where did you feel it? How would you describe the sensation? Repeat this same set of questions with an unsuccessful decision.

Example #1: You've got a sales call to make. You've been dreading this call all morning. At around 11:30 you feel an odd surge of energy in your body and decide to pick up the phone and make the call. It turns out you reached the client at just the right time and she was happy to hear from you.

Example #2: You wake up on Tuesday morning. The thought "I should get into the office early today" pops into your mind. You override this idea by telling yourself you'll work late instead. You notice your stomach hurts. As you pull out onto the highway, you hear the traffic reporter for your radio station announce major delays on your route to work. If you had left 30 minutes prior, you would have avoided it all.

Begin to check in with your body when making small decisions.

Who should I call to get background on this issue?

Is this a good time to make that phone call?

Is it important for me to be at that meeting?

Which restaurant should I choose?

Should I work with Joe or Mary on this project?

Which book would be most helpful in getting up to speed on this topic?

It might be a good idea to keep a journal of your decisions. What was the decision? How did it feel in your body? Was it a good, bad, or neutral decision? When you become comfortable with the way you receive insight on small decisions, you'll be surprised at the speed with which you'll be able to get accurate intuitive information on larger decisions.

What's Got Your Attention?

If something keeps nudging you and you can't get it out of your mind, take some steps towards the idea. You don't have to know the whole path or the destination. Trust that your intuition is guiding you via the next step to take.

It's Normal to Feel Uncertain

Very few people feel 100-percent confident that they have the right stuff to reach their goal. If they're honest, most will tell you that they feel scared, feel fearful, and lack confidence a good part of the time. Figure out a strategy or philosphy that keeps you going when your conviction wavers. Possibilities include talking to a mentor or a coach. It could also come through inspirational reading and through a spiritual faith.

Shake Things Up

When you're feeling insecure and uncertain, you usually want to stay in your comfort zone. Who wants more uncertainty?! Resoundingly, successful gut trusters said they had to move beyond safe, routine, and secure activities. What does that look like? Email someone you've admired and ask for their advice. (I had to do that many times for this book.) Take a class in a field related to your interest. Introduce yourself to a stranger at a meeting or party. When you begin to do this, you'll put yourself in the milieu where connections and opportunities can occur. You'll be surprised at the number of helpful folks out there in the world.

Ignore the Rules

There will be a lot of naysayers when you learn to trust your gut. "You can't do that." "It's not done that way." "To succeeed in business, you need to_____ ____." The successful business people of tomorrow will be the ones who did things differently today. They trusted their instincts and created new rules—ones that work for them. If you fail, consider it a detour. Learn from your mistakes, pick yourself back up, and move forward again. If you aren't experiencing setbacks at least some of the time, you're not truly trying new things.

Make a List of Your Choices

Get out a pad of paper. Think about your goal or intention. In can be an intangible one such as wanting more fun or happiness. It could also be a tangible goal such as a job with a specific title, salary, or industry. Now write down a dozen or more possible courses of action you could take to meet this goal. After you've finished your list, step back and take a look.

Which one leaps out at you and makes you want to begin right now? That's your intuitive answer. Now go do it!

Put Your Intuition to Work Tip
Your body has information that may lie just below your conscious awareness. The next time you're faced with a decision, large or small, check in with your body. Does an option you're considering feel *off*, or *right*, in your belly? Are there other physical clues that might indicate a right, or wrong decision?

Chapter 6 | Listen to Your Inner CEO

Your Inner CEO can help you generate income streams, create opportunities, find people, build your business, maximize your profits, increase your income, solve problems, and improve your quality of life in ways you can't even imagine now.

—Robert Sheinfeld, author of *The 11th Element*

David Becker is an angel investor to startups and is a big fan of trusting his intuition. He calls it his "Inner Consultant," and in my 2015 interview with him, he credited it with saving his former company. At the time of the story that follows, he was CEO of Philippe Becker Design (PBD), a branding and packaging agency:

We had been named the fifth fastest growing company in San Francisco. Our clients included Disney, Forbes, Gap, Safeway, T-Mobile, Whole Foods Market, and Williams-Sonoma, Inc.

We were in dire need of a key financial person for our rapidly growing firm. This was a major hire for us that would enable us to get to the next level of growth. We'd spent a great deal of time searching for the right person. Obviously they needed to be a good fit in terms of credentials. But it was also important to us that whoever we hired be an equally good fit for our culture, beliefs, and business approach.

The person we homed in on seemed to meet all the major criteria. Everything clicked. Everyone was in agreement. Frankly, I was so desperate to get that person on board, I was like a kid who wants a bike for Christmas. That's how great the desire was to hire him and get him started.

At the same time I began to recognize that something was gnawing at me about this person. I can only describe it as a danger signal. Something at the back of my mind kept niggling at me. This was someone who would have access to all of our financial information. It was an extremely important position in my company and everyone was looking to me to be the final decision-maker.

I realized I didn't have my emotions in check about this key decision. I was a little too excited. That was part of the warning for me. I decided to do a routine background check via the Internet. Somewhat to my surprise, nothing untoward showed up about this man. Yet I still didn't feel right.

I decided to go through a process that I learned while getting my MBA. I separated the decision making into three different segments. The first was my logical analysis of this person's viability. Second was my emotional state about wanting him to be the right hire. Third was my raw, unadulterated intuition. When I was able to take out the emotion and logic, I was able to see that something was still wrong.

I realized that I had allowed emotion to overpower my gut feelings. That, combined with the excitement of thinking I had found the right person and having his credentials check out. After this exercise I was still left with a sense of unease. I decided to spend several thousand dollars to do a more thorough background investigation. I received the results the next day. They confirmed my instincts. He had been convicted of several felonious acts involving company funds in another state. Hiring him would have been a disaster.

The process David ultimately used to make his decision brings to mind a quote found on ThinkExist.com by English mystery writer Margery Allingham. She writes about one of her characters, "He did not arrive at this conclusion by the decent process of quiet, logical deduction, nor yet by the blinding flash of glorious intuition, but by the shoddy, untidy process halfway between the two by which one usually gets to know things."

Your Inner Consultant Wants to Help

There is part of you that knows the best direction toward success in any endeavor. Think of this as your "Inner Consultant." If you were to hire a real-life, flesh-and-blood consultant, you'd want to have a meeting to discuss your concerns. You'd also have some questions for this consultant. Try this technique when you need some answers to any of life's dilemmas.

To make the best use of this exercise, set aside 10 to 20 minutes where you'll be undisturbed. You'll need to write down any information you receive. Use a computer, smartphone, or a notebook to jot notes. You may find the responses come easily if you sit quietly for a few minutes. Others have found it best to sit at their keyboard and simply write whatever comes to mind. The intuitive answers may also come to you when you least expect them!

Make a statement about what you want and then ask an open-ended question. Here are some ideas to get you started:

I'd like to create record breaking sales this quarter. What is the best way to do this?

I want to motivate my product development team. What's a good approach?

I want to feel excited by my career again. What are some options that would work for me?

I'd like to improve my ability to listen to my intuition. What steps should I take?

As always with intuitive messages, the answers may come as an idea, a fully formed thought, a symbolic image, a physical sensation, or a fleeting impression. Jot down or draw whatever answers come. Expect further information to arrive within the next day or two. Look at your answers from time to time and see how the intuitive intelligence you received has shifted your thoughts in new directions.

Create Some "White Space" in Your Life

Libby Wagner is a poet, author, and speaker, and one of the only former poetry professors warmly invited into the boardroom. Libby is a trusted advisor for presidents, CEOs, and executive directors, and her work has shaped the cultures of numerous Fortune 500 clients, including The Boeing Company, Nike, Philips, SAP, Diageo, and Costco. Using her unique approach, Libby helps executives create dramatic, memorable impact so they confidently lead their organizations toward innovative horizons.

She does what a lot of consultants do, which is change companies, improve their leadership and communication, and increase creativity and innovation. However, the way she gets there is very different. In my interview with her, she describes how intuition is hugely important in her process. She brings what she calls a "Poetic Paradigm" to the individuals or groups she works with. Libby says:

We're helping leaders find their voice and clearly articulate a vision to bring about positive change in their organizations. We do that by helping them listen deeply within. What does poetry have to do with business?

When working with clients, I'll write the following words up on the board:

Courage

Noticing

Remembering your humanity

Specificity

I ask, "When do you need to use these?" Of course, people respond that they need and use these all the time. These are the same skills a poet uses.

The first two steps of any kind of process I take people through is:

1. Letting go
2. Listening deeply

By listening deeply you're making space for the good stuff to come. You're listening to your internal self—your intuition. You're also paying close attention and noticing around you. You may notice people, something that shows up or something that happens.

I'm asking that people let go of knowing something in their head and listen deeply to what their inner wisdom is saying. It involves slowing down. It's counterintuitive to almost all the other messages we receive in our organizations, which is to increase the speed.

When you're being present in the here and now, you're aware of much more that's happening around you. If you drop back six steps, what do you see, what do you hear or what do you feel? It's all about noticing. It's hard to pay attention to your intuition if you're moving too quickly. That's the thing we need to push against in order to be able to cultivate presence and connect to our intuitive powers. If we're overworked and overwhelmed and worshiping at the church of busyness, we don't hear it.

Libby recommends creating what she calls "white space" in your daily life. She thinks of these as a space without an agenda. These are brief moments of unscheduled time throughout the day. She suggests using them to look up at the clouds, take a walk, close your eyes, and breathe, or simply daydream. It's all about taking the time to listen. It's about slowing down, and being open to life and the inner wisdom that resides in us all.

Libby gives her clients a blank journal and asks them to write with a pen, rather than a keyboard, to encourage inspiration and intuition. During these "white space" times, she suggests they jot down any ideas, feelings, or "a-ha" moments and capture them on the page. She says:

Listen for questions that don't go away and conversations that need to take place. You're asking for visible and invisible help. You're paying attention to the whispers you're receiving as well as what is going on around you.

When you don't pay attention to the intuitive information you're receiving, life tends to hit you over the head with the proverbial two-by-four to get your attention. That's when I hear people say, "I knew I should have done something different" or "I had a feeling I didn't make the right choice." It's all about honing that inner wisdom and taking action on the information one receives.

The Low-Tech Way to Gather Intuitive Intelligence

A colleague of mine had an interesting variation on Libby's method. He was a decidedly "low-tech" kind of guy. He wrote a question to his Inner Consultant on a 3-x-5 card every morning. He kept the card in his shirt pocket. He explains that, throughout the day, he writes flashes of insight, "thought messages," and coincidences relevant to his question. He feels that having them in his pocket keeps him attuned to the questions and open to the answers.

I ran into him recently at a speech I gave. He showed me a stack of his cards that represented several days worth of inquiry. They were filled with creative information and wisdom that he credits with helping him increase sales, hire good employees, and successfully resolve a difficult issue with one of his biggest clients. "I couldn't survive without my cards. They're my second brain!" he said with a laugh.

Intuition Can Provide Unique Insight

Your Inner Consultant is the creative part of your mind that answers when you ask a question such as "I wonder how else I can look at this problem?" or "I wonder how else I could deal with this decision?" or "I wonder what other possibilities exist to solve this problem?"

Justin Brady is the owner of Cultivate, an agency that connects highly creative and innovative companies to elusive markets. He speaks to leadership teams about creative methodology and has written for numerous publications including

The *Washington Post,* The *Wall Street Journal*, and *Forbes*. I spoke with him by phone in December 2015 about how he uses intuition with his clients. According to Justin:

Much of my work revolves around connecting cutting edge companies to elusive markets that will benefit from their product. Many times, this product is so cutting edge, it's difficult to communicate to the audience that can benefit because there hasn't been anything like it before, or the product is met with a "yea, right" response.

Because little research is ever available in this scenario, much of my success relies on the intuition I have developed over time: The ability to understand what a client's subconscious mind is trying to communicate when they don't fully understand it themselves. Also, determining the difference between what they think their client needs and what their client really needs.

I've discovered I can increase my intuitive perception by listening to every little word and sigh, and paying very close attention to body language and even small talk. Most times we try to be objective and only write down the words we hear, but when we do that, we are missing the subtle cues our subconscious brain has picked up on.

My intuition training is responsible for discovering unique ways to connect a client's innovative ideas to people in a way that is meaningful for both parties, creating lasting business relationships. Many know intuition is important, but many don't know that you can improve it by just slowing down and listening.

> **Put Your Intuition to Work Tip**
> Your "Inner Consultant" is the creative part of your mind that answers when you ask outcome-oriented questions such as "How else could I look at this issue?" or "What could I do to get the results I want?" or even, "What would X [favorite expert] do?"

| | | Put Your Intuition to Work Technique | | |
The Intuitive Ideas Log

Whether you're keeping a journal or writing as a meditation, it's the same thing. What's important is you're having a relationship with your mind.

—Natalie Goldberg, author of *Writing Down the Bones*

Developing intuition is like developing any other skill. The more you use it the better you get at it. Keeping an intuition journal is a terrific way to expand your proficiency. Keep your ideas written in one place, whether it's on your phone or computer, or in a notebook.

Many people have found it helpful to create "intuition check-in" points during the day. This is a time set aside, often at the beginning of the workday, to check in with their intuition.

Sit in a quiet place or simply close the door to your office and hold your calls.

Consider your concerns, issues, decisions, and challenges for the day. Write them out in your journal. Give each one a separate page.

Close your eyes and take several slow, deep breaths, and center yourself.

Bring each of your concerns to mind one-by-one. Ask questions such as "What should I know about…?" Or make a statement such as "I need information about…."

Pay attention to intuitive response(s). Remember: Intuition doesn't usually come in fully formed sentences. A picture, phrase, feeling, or a symbolic image can be equally valuable.

Write all responses—even brief fragments—into your journal. Try not to edit or analyze your answers during this exercise. That can come later.

Don't be discouraged if you're not immediately flooded with insightful wisdom. Intuitive insights have a way of arriving when you least expect them, often coming to mind later in the day. When a great idea comes, make a note of it! An intuition journal is a way to invite more and more valuable hunches and instincts.

Check back with it frequently. You may find that an answer that didn't make sense earlier in the month provides exactly the information you need now.

Chapter 7 | Intuition Can Help You Find Your Calling

If you find what you do each day seems to have no link to any higher purpose, you probably want to rethink what you're doing.
—Ronald A. Heifetz, author of *The Practice of Adaptive Leadership*

Idan Shpizear has a zeal about life and business that's contagious. He's the co-founder and CEO of 911 Restoration, a company that helps homeowners recover from water, fire, and other disasters. In my Ocotober 2015 phone interview with him, he describes how intuition is a big part of his success story. In 2003, he moved to the United States from Israel with his friend Peleg Lindenberg. They each came with $1,500 in their pocket and shared a tiny apartment with five guys. They began a carpet cleaning business out of an old, beat-up Volvo. Idan says, "We didn't know the language. We couldn't even read the street signs to know whether we had parked the Volvo in a No Parking zone. But I had a dream and I knew I was meant to pursue it."

He describes a deep yearning to do something bigger with his life and wanting to make a positive impact on others through his business. At first, he says, it was all about making money. But he recognized that the bigger desire was about what he could bring to the world: "It was a process of self-discovery, of deep, inner guidance. I call it being 'Aligned.' It pulls you forward."

He realized that simply cleaning carpets wasn't enough. Idan says:

Where is the opportunity? Where is the right place to go? I trusted that belief I had in myself and in that larger dream. I thought that if I could dream it, I could create it. I believe we all have this inner dream. When you become aligned, you wake up. You don't fall back to sleep, lulling yourself with negative self-talk, telling yourself you're a failure and won't make it. You face those fears. We all have them. Instead of running away from them, go into them and embrace them.

The fears are simply what you're telling yourself from a limited place in your mind. It's stuff you make up to scare yourself so you have an excuse to not do the thing you're meant to do. When you can get into that feeling of being aligned with that bigger dream, you allow yourself more openness. Things like meditation, taking time for self-reflection, and reading inspirational books all help. They allow you to see your life and experiences with different eyes.

The thing you want, the bigger dream, it exists inside you. You just have to tune into it, asking, "Do I want to move forward? Am I willing to do this? Can I embrace it even if it takes me through some difficult times?"

That's how Idan described this process that took him from cleaning carpets to the larger dream of helping people have a "fresh start" after devastating events caused damage or destruction to their homes and businesses.

Idan has followed his inner wisdom throughout his life. It guides him to his next steps, helps him come up with new products and assists him in motivating his franchise owners as well as elementary school kids whom he coaches to follow their dreams. He describes his daily practice as rising early, taking time for meditation, writing, and reflection. "It's all about your own development," he says. It sounds so simple. Yet it's taken Idan from a modest beginning of $3,000 to 60 offices all around the country. It's what anyone would describe as an impressive success.

What Are You Here to Do?

Oprah Winfrey would seem to be agreeing with Idan when she wrote in the November 2010 South Africa issue of *O Magazine*, "Ignoring your passion is like dying a slow death....

Passion whispers to you through your feelings, beckoning you toward your highest good. Pay attention to what makes you feel energized, connected, and stimulated. It's what gives you your juice. Do what you love; give it back in the form of service, and you will do more than succeed. You will triumph."

We all have times in our lives when we feel stuck and bored. The job that was so exciting and promising when we accepted the position is now anything but. One client referred to this as feeling he had "run of the edge off the map" he had created for his life.

Janet was a client who came to me for an intuitive session. She was in what most would describe as an enviable position. She was the COO for a leading and fast-growing technology company. Janet says:

I used to love everything about this job, including the fast pace, the rapid change, having to keep up with all the latest and greatest technology and still being on the leading edge of that expertise. I was an adrenaline junky. The more that got thrown at me, the faster I went.

I ascended the corporate ladder very quickly and here I am today with what should be my dream job. The problem is, it no longer excites me. To be honest, I'm exhausted. I used to thrive on all the corporate politics that enabled me to reach this position. Now I'm finding it all kind of petty and sad. I want to leave, to do something different—more service-oriented—but how do I begin? I don't have a clear vision of what's next.

It's times like these that author and Jungian analyst Jean Shinoda Bolen, MD, wrote about. There's a great quote from her on ThinkExist.com: "You have the need and the right to spend part of your life caring for your soul. It is not easy. You have to resist the demands of the work-oriented, often defensive, element in your psyche that measures life only in terms of output—how much you produce—not in terms of the quality of your life experiences."

Knowing When It's Time for a Change

Almost all of us wish that our intuition would speak with a loud voice saying, in effect, "Here is your next big mission. Go for it now!" Instead, when we're tired, exhausted, and jaded like Janet, it tends to whisper things like:

- Take some time off.
- Reduce your workload; delegate.
- Write in your journal.
- Talk to a coach, counselor, or an intuitive.
- Rest when you're weary.
- Meditate.
- Reflect.
- Read inspirational books.
- Go on a retreat.
- Hang out with friends who "get" you.
- Spend time in nature.
- Sleep, rest, and recharge.

Those things are usually not the areas that goal-seeking action-takers want to pay attention to, and yet they really are the crucial next step. It helps to think of it as part of a natural cycle. During this time, you are planting the seeds for the next growth cycle in your life. It's a time of rest and hibernation, of waiting and trusting that what you're planting will come to fruition when the time and circumstances are right.

As Janet's session came to a close, she agreed to two things:

1. She would take a period of six months to explore options. She wanted to drop the pressure to make a decision right now.

2. She would begin to employ some of the "slow down" ideas above and some of the questions below in order to dream and reflect on the new life she wanted to create for herself.

Questions to Ask Yourself

The following questions are great ones to spend some time with. Intuitive information comes to most people more easily when using old-fashioned paper and pen rather than a computer. Experiment with whatever works best for you. Find some uninterrupted quiet time and think about the following questions. If you feel excited or curious about an idea or answer, follow that. It's your inner wisdom communicating with you.

What are you yearning for? The answer to this is more likely to elicit an adjective (such as *connection, fun, meaning, adventure,* or *peace*) rather than a specific goal.

What are you doing when time seems to fly by?

Perhaps your ideal job might exist or be created within your present company. If you were offered the ideal job what would it be?

What do you look forward to doing on the weekends or on a vacation?

When you think of someone who has a "dream job," what do they do?

If money were no object, what kind of work would you love to do?

If your boss told you she'd give you a year off to contribute to the community in some way, what would you choose to do?

Are there any classes you might like to take at the local college or adult education center?

Close your eyes. Take a deep breath and relax. What images come to mind as you see yourself in your ideal work?

What is your intuition communicating to you right now about your ideal job?

Is there any action that you're being guided to take? Is there anything that feels exciting, compelling, or interesting that you want to act on? You may not receive insight on the ultimate end goal, simply the right next step.

The Strong Pull of What You Love

Catherine Booth was the founder of the Salvation Army. She expressed the thought that "We are made for larger ends than Earth can encompass. Let us be true to our exalted destiny." What can you do to become clear about that destiny? The first step in creating anything new is to have some ideas about what you want. One of the poet Rumi's famous lines is "Let yourself be silently drawn by the stronger pull of what you really love."

Sometimes we get stuck in our own way. Our logical brains tell us we "don't know" what to do. Or we "just don't know" our life purpose. Or we "just don't know" how we could ever earn a living at this! Following is a great sentence completion exercise that I love: "Wouldn't it be great if…?" You fill in the blank with whatever your heart desires. Grab a pad of paper and complete as many of those sentences as you can think of.

Examples:

Wouldn't it be great if:

A wonderful, fun job came my way?

I could make a living doing _____?

I discovered my calling was _____?

It will take some focus, insight, and practice to begin thinking in this new and expanded way. You may have to take it as a matter of trust that your intuition will be able to deliver some brilliant new ideas. It also helps to be receptive to synchronicities and coincidences that will open up possibilities and new directions.

I realize that any of these ideas is not necessarily going to evoke instant clarity about either your vocation or your life mission, but it's a start! Every single person who is living a life they love had to begin by asking themselves questions like these. They also had to believe in themselves enough to take the risks to move in the direction of their dreams. You don't need to quit your day job right now. You simply need to begin spending more time doing what you love, reaching out to others who might be able to help you create your dream, and continuing to dream a little bigger with each step forward.

This is not the place to worry about practicality or to concern yourself with how in the world you'll make money at your calling. Simply think about what a life you love would look like in the areas of relationships with others, work, money, spiritual life, belongings, home, family, achievements, health, education, free time, hobbies, and travel.

Trust That the Answers Will Come

How does all of this merge into a calling? As always, the answers will come in a variety of forms. Confusion and mystery are somewhat the hallmarks of a calling. There are hints, inner whispers, nudges, and something akin to puzzle pieces to put together. Also, be aware that there may not be one big "life purpose" or mission. That's entirely acceptable. Your life may be made up of a series of callings that change and develop as you age.

As you listen within, what are you compelled to act on? It may be a feeling of curiosity about something. It could show itself as a book you suddenly want to read, a memory of something you loved as a child, or a thought to call someone you haven't seen in a while. As always, small steps are as important as large ones. Again from ThinkExist.com, Jean Shinoda Bolen, MD, has wisdom to share on this topic: "Before you can do something that you've never done before, you have to be able to imagine it's possible." It's time to begin dreaming and imagining.

Put Your Intuition to Work Tip
What are you curious about? What compels or interests you? As you follow the answers to those questions and the ones in this chapter, you will be directed to your intuitively guided next steps. Pieces of the puzzle of your life will begin to line up.

| | | Put Your Intuition to Work Technique | | |
What Are You Ready to Act On?

I believe that every minute we're awake our life is sending us messages about what we should be doing, where we should be headed.

—Eileen Fisher

Sometimes you become confused because you can't figure out how to get from where you are to where you want to go. You may also feel stuck because something doesn't feel right. This is when your intuition can help. Maybe all that's required is a small step, not a huge leap. Quite often when you take a step forward, more information becomes available to you.

Many people report that, as they make an intuitive choice toward what proves to be a correct decision, events begin flowing easily, doors to opportunity open, and coincidences begin to occur.

Which of the following feels like the next best step?

I need to gather more information.

I'd like to call _____ and ask for her input.

This decision should be delayed.

I'm ready to act on _____ but not _____.

I'd like to make a list of pros and cons.

I'd like to ask _____ and _____ to brainstorm with me.

I'm not comfortable with the direction we're headed and need to slow this down.

What small step(s) can you take today?

Chapter 8 | Listen With an Open Mind and Heart

Listening is a magnetic and strange thing, a creative force. The friends who listen to us are the ones we move toward. When we are listened to, it creates us, makes us unfold and expand.

—Karl A. Menniger, American psychiatrist

Jason is the director of sales for a national pharmaceutical company. His regional sales manager, Sally, walked into his office. She was concerned about one of their biggest customers and began a detailed overview of the problem. Jason had a big day in front of him with lots of meetings, making him impatient to get a resolution to Sally's issue. His mind was racing. He became a bit annoyed with her for not offering some solutions. As his impatience grew, he blurted out a quick response and hoped that it sufficed. He rushed off to his next meeting, leaving Sally looking distraught.

Later in the day, when Jason had a little more time to think, he realized that his reaction to Sally was hasty and probably not that helpful. He knows that she's a strong sales manager and deserved his time and attention, especially when a major client was involved. He resolved to do things differently next time. He wanted to be a leader who listens with his mind and *heart*, not to necessarily come up with a logical yes or no, do-or-don't-do answer.

Management consultant Peter Drucker provided wise advice, found on BrainyQuote.com: "The most important thing in communication is hearing what isn't said." Jason committed to learning that skill and reported months later that the idea had helped him change the whole dynamic on his team in a very positive direction.

The Power of the Open-Ended Question

Similar to Drucker, Benjamin Franklin once suggested it was best to "Speak little, do much." This could apply to the power of intuitive listening. Good managers usually talk less and listen more. In fact, people who have been defined as "great bosses" by their subordinates simply ask good questions. They hire competent, smart people, and then trust their staff to resolve issues and come up with good solutions. The questions they ask are more like coaching than problem-solving. They welcome their employees to think more freely, creatively, and intuitively.

People report that when they can talk about their problem out loud without interruption, they can often resolve the issue on their own. Open-ended questions can encourage conversation and expand the depth of possible solutions.

What are good open-ended questions? They are usually ones that don't require a "yes" or "no" answer. They promote dialogue and allow the person being questioned to expand on their thinking and come up with outside-of-the-box solutions. It also allows the manager to more deeply understand the challenges facing the individual or the department.

Here are some examples that Jason decided to use both with Sally and with his other direct reports:

What's been happening since our last meeting?

I'm curious about that. Could you tell me more?

What kind of challenges are you facing?

Could you tell me more about your observations?

What's your most important priority regarding this issue?

What outcome do you want to have (with this person or situation) and what could you do to achieve that?

What do you think would be a good next step?

What kind of support do you need in order to accomplish this?

What other issues are important to you?

What else?

What's the most important thing I can do for you?

What was most helpful to you about this conversation?

You may find other open-ended questions that work for you depending on the issues you're trying to address. You may find the best ones in the other person's response to the final question in the previous list.

How to Listen Intuitively

Good questions are a great start in having a deeper understanding of both an individual and the issues at hand. But how can you also listen just as deeply? In the midst of any conversation, our left brain is busy trying to come up with answer. It's thinking of the next question. It's judging your behavior and the other persons. You are usually hyper-aware of how we're being perceived and if you're doing everything "right." It's amazing the things that go on in our minds during the course of a normal conversation!

When you're listening intuitively, you're paying attention with your body, heart, and mind. You're listening for the whole message the person is conveying. Information may come to you through a body sensation. For example, you may feel your gut tighten if something feels "off" or wrong to you. You may also be aware of the tone of the person's voice or their expression. Is it matching what they're saying? When you access your intuitive information in this way, you're more compassionate. You can hear the critical data that the person is conveying as well as how they feel and their deeper, yet unspoken, concerns.

For example, in the conversation with Sally, Jason was aware that he had not been helpful to her. When reflecting back on it, he noted that at the end of the meeting, she looked anxious. She was saying, "Okay. I understand. I agree," while shaking her head back and forth as if saying, "No. I don't agree or understand." Jason mentioned that he *felt* something he described as an emptiness or a let-down feeling as he walked out of the office to his next meeting.

Dr. Marcia Reynolds is a leadership coach, president of Covisioning LLC, and author of *The Discomfort Zone: How Leaders Turn Difficult Conversations Into Breakthroughs.* She's fascinated by the brain, especially what triggers enthusiasm and innovation. In our October 2015 Skype interview, she joked that in her spare time she accumulates degrees. Her doctoral degree is in organizational development. This fascination has led her down many roads in her desire to stay on top of the shifts in employee engagement and leadership development.

On this journey, she wove together three areas of expertise: organizational change, coaching, and emotional intelligence. She is able to draw on these areas as she works with her latest passion: changing the conversations leaders have at work. She feels the most effective leaders help people think more broadly for themselves. When leaders have powerful conversations that change people's minds from the inside out, the workplace comes alive with an eagerness to discover what is possible. She believes that these conversations emerge when leaders listen to their intuition.

How does she convey this? "I found that using your intuition means listening with your entire nervous system, including your heart and gut as well as your brain." She relates that most of us don't listen well because we're paying attention to the part of our brain that's judging, censoring, and chatting away trying to think of what to say next. When we're focused there, we're not paying attention to what's happening in our heart and gut.

She says, "Listening is complex. When you listen to someone from your head, you hear their assumptions and beliefs that frame their version of the story. From your heart, you are able to sense what they desire, why they feel cheated or disappointed and why they are cynical or upset. From your gut, you sense what they are afraid of, including what they are attached to. You receive input from your entire nervous system if you are open to receiving this information."

Dr. Reynolds suggests accessing your intuition before you speak. It helps to stay grounded in the present moment. "Intuition is not from outer space; it's from inner space." To access your intuition, you are learning to listen beyond the spoken word. You need to feel grounded in the present moment and visualize opening all the centers in your neural network. Use curiosity to open your mind. Compassion and a desire to be helpful are needed to open your heart. Courage is required to trust your gut. It allows you to say the often-difficult things people need to hear. She suggests that before you speak, think of someone or something you deeply care about to open your heart and then say the word *courage* to yourself as you breathe in deeply to open all three centers.

Reynolds observed that, depending on your personality, you may find it easier to access your heart over your gut, or vice versa. People who tend to be helpers listen more easily from their heart. Conversely, folks who are risk-takers and action-oriented find it much easier to listen to their gut. It may help you when communicating with others to consciously pay attention to both, and open the area that you find weakest.

Marcia acknowledges that listening with an open mind, heart, and gut takes conscious and consistent practice. If you take time each day to actively listen from these three centers, you'll open and develop your intuition. People around you will feel heard and understood. Ultimately, these listening and conversing skills make for a happier and more successful team.

The Intuitive Conversation

In the words of Malcolm Forbes, on Forbes.com, "The art of conversation lies in listening." So how do you become a good listener and not just a problem solver? Read on for a few tips.

Keep the Focus on Them

People who come to us for advice often simply need to vent. It helps them get clear about their own emotions, ideas, and intentions. Resist the urge to immediately jump in with your advice and personal experiences, especially at the beginning of the conversation. Often all that's needed is to listen with empathy and understanding. Think about using some of the questions listed above to help the person discover their own inner answers.

Pay Attention to Communication Style

As reported on BusinessBalls.com, researchers have found that only 7 percent of communication involves actual words. In fact, 55 percent of communication is visual and 38 percent is vocal. The former includes eye contact and body language. The latter includes the tone and pitch of your voice as well as how fast or slow you speak. You're always communicating through your facial expressions and body posture as well as your voice. Think of a time you tried to communicate something important to someone and they had their arms crossed with a frown on their face. Not too welcoming! What could you do to convey a warm, open, and encouraging atmosphere during an important conversation? Similar to Marcia Reynolds's techniques, it may take a little practice at first.

Keep Your Mind Open

It's all too easy to leap to conclusions when you hear someone's story. However, be sensitive to the fact that everyone views the world a little differently. They have skills, strengths, weaknesses, and ideas that are likely quite dissimilar to yours. It doesn't make them right or wrong—just different. As they're relating their story, understand that it could be based on inaccurate or inconclusive information. Your task is to listen as openly as possible without judgment to help you and the speaker gain more clarity.

Notice Your Own Intuition

While you're having a conversation, pay attention to what's going on in your body and emotions. There's great wisdom there that we often don't tap into. Perhaps something made you feel sad, upset, or angry, or the person responded in an unusual way given the circumstances, or something was said that didn't add up. It's possible that you weren't even conscious of exactly what caught your attention. With practice, you'll notice these things in a way that you can then bring to your conscious attention and to the conversation for further exploration. When something makes you tense, uncomfortable, or simply curious, pay attention. There's probably something just beneath the surface. The easiest way to address this is by saying such things as "I'd like to check something out with you" or "I'm wondering if…." You're basically asking the speaker to elaborate so you can both gain clarity.

Intuition and open intuitive listening are powerful tools in any relationship. It helps build rapport and encourages self-awareness and trust—important outcomes in business or in your personal life.

> **P**ut Your Intuition to Work Tip
> Listen more and give advice less. Ask open-ended questions that begin with "what" or "how." It's one of the best ways to open up the conversation to intuitive insight and wisdom.

{ }

Chapter 9 | Take an Insight Break

Your calm mind is the ultimate weapon against your challenges. So relax.
—Bryant McGill, author and founder of Good Will Treaty for World Peace

We're often so swept up in our professional roles that we rush from meeting to phone call to e-mail and back again, and we don't take time for even a brief break. However, I believe that reverie is crucial to the intuitive mind. I found clear evidence of this while writing this very chapter. I had nailed the beginning, and had come up with an exercise and the story you'll read here. I then found myself staring at the page, editing the same sentence over and over. The dreaded writer's block!

I decided to go for a walk and simply ask my creative mind, "What do I need to write for this chapter?" By the time I'd completed a stroll around my neighborhood, I had several solid ideas that seemed worthy to write about. (I hope you'll agree.)

When you're overwhelmed and feeling stymied and blocked, making yourself work harder is usually counterproductive. Your creativity dries up; the numbers you're trying to crunch swim before your eyes. The intuitive insight you need just isn't coming to you. The solution? When you're besieged and need answers, take a hike.

Is there a place near your office that makes you feel calm? Go there the next time you need insight. The answers you receive during those 30 minutes will be more than equal to the hours of statistics and analysis you had planned.

When you get there, begin to stroll. Focus on the present. Use all your senses and take in all that is around you. Notice the fragrance in the air, the sounds of the birds, and the breeze on your skin. Take some slow, deep breaths. Observe how you feel.

As you become calmer, think about what has been disturbing your peace of mind. Frame it into a question as you continue your walk and listen for answers.

Intuitive insights come to you more easily when you're relaxed and have an open state of mind.

Ask questions.

The answers will come.

Let the Ideas "Pop"

I spoke with Jon Schallert by phone in October 2015. Jon is a professional speaker and business consultant specializing in teaching businesses how to turn themselves into "Consumer Destinations. Jon speaks to thousands annually about his "Destination Business" process. His methodology has been used extensively by towns, cities, and seasonal tourist locations as well as independent small business owners.

His work requires him to be on the road a lot, driving between small towns that might not be served by a regional airport. He says:

This is often where I get my best ideas! I keep a pad of paper and pen beside me and I drive without listening to music. I think about what I want to accomplish at my next event, in my business or my life in general.

I find that ideas just pop into my head. "I should be doing this!" or "Why the heck am I doing that?" I write it all down, often pulling over to the side of the road when I get a particularly spectacular idea so I can capture it all.

When I get to my destination, I read through all my notes and apply my logical brain. The ones that leap out at me—the ones I'm excited about—are the ideas I consider intuitively guided. Then I ask myself, "What can I implement immediately? What needs some work?" I get more great, successful ideas with this method than months of research and strategizing.

Jon said something else interesting that was touched on by a number of folks I interviewed:

When something I'm working on gets really difficult, I've learned to step back from it to wait and/or reassess.

I'm not talking about the normal problems one experiences all the time in business. It's the ones where you get really weird obstacles in multiple ways that tend to cause things to continually fall apart.

I try to view those situations as ones where something better or more positive wants to emerge. If I can refrain from pushing my own ego-driven agenda, a new direction, idea, or outcome often comes about.

He gives this as an example: Jon and his wife, Peg, wanted to downsize from their large home outside of Denver, Colorado, to a smaller place in the mountains where they could cross-country ski. He says:

We found a great cabin we liked and put an offer on it. Without belaboring the details, we experienced one weird complication after another. We finally withdrew our offer.

We still needed a place in the city where I could present my Destination Boot Camp. We also needed a place to stay when I had to get to the airport during the times that the roads to the mountains were snowed in.

We ended up finding this amazing 140-year-old bank building. It wasn't even on the market. But the owner was willing to sell. It had a terrific apartment upstairs that Peg and I could live in. It was perfect. Every visionary in the city had walked through the doors to this place at one time or another. Great history!

Right after we bought it, we found another cabin in the mountains. This one was even better than the last one. Best of all, the purchase and sale of both buildings all happened seamlessly this time. I just had to get out of the way and let things be easy. It's amazing the energy that "going with the flow" can release.

Find Sources of Inspiration

Many of the people I interviewed for this book had similar "allowing things to happen" strategies. Here's a sampling of other ways interviewees invoke intuitive insight at work:

- I subscribe to an "inspirational quote" e-newsletter. I print out the quote and post it where I can view it throughout the day. It helps keep me focused on what life is all about.

- Before I start my day, I read a verse from the Bible or other inspirational book.

- I make it a priority to eat lunch in a nearby park or, in inclement weather, even in my car. I find after I return to my desk I have a huge burst of creativity.

- I go to the gym for a half hour during my workday. Working out gets the cobwebs out of my brain and I come up with wonderful ideas while running on the treadmill or lifting weights.

- My company has a meditation room. I go there for reflection and prayer as part of my lunch break. I come back to work feeling centered and relaxed. The answers to issues I was struggling with in the morning seem to be resolved during that brief time for contemplation.

- If I can't actually get away from the office, I make a point of changing my location. It can often be as simple as switching from my desk to the couch in my office. The minor change helps me maintain my mental alertness and increases my productivity. I actually think of it as my "inspiration couch."

- I bring my laptop to the park. Nothing like a change of scenery to fire up my creative juices.

⊦ I reserve time in our company conference room several times a week. It looks out onto a huge field filled with wildflowers. I use those occasions as my intuition time. I bring a notepad, colored pens and pencils, and do some creative mind-mapping. I get amazing results fast.

⊦ I block off 'intuition time" in my calendar each day. These are a few sacred minutes where I have unscheduled time to stare out the window, day-dream and rest my brain. It makes my often crazy days seem so much saner!

The "intuitive break" strategy I heard echoed most often was from those who confessed they took a nap at work. Surprisingly, a vast majority of executives and entrepreneurs alike confessed that it was one of the quickest ways they found to make a decision or come up with a solution.

Take a Power Nap

According to Dr. Sara Mednick, a research scientist at the prestigious Salk Institute for Biological Studies in La Jolla, California, the benefits of even a brief 20-minute nap are pro-found. ExecutiveStyle.com.au reports the results of a study that shows that naps result in "greater alertness, improved memory retention and creative insight."

There's evidence that many companies are catching on to the idea of napping in the workplace. Some of these include Google, Huffington Post, Zappos, Pizza Hut, and Ben & Jerry's. There's even a company called "MetroNaps" that leases "nap pods" to businesses with sleep-deprived employ-ees. They began in 2003 and now are in dozens of countries across four continents.

Yarde Metals Inc. in Bristol, Connecticut, is a metals distribution company that built a 2,000-square-foot "nap room" in each of their facilities. Each of them is large enough to accommodate 20 employees at a time.

According to a February 2013 article on BBC.com, a study claims that 30 percent of employees come up with their best, most creative ideas as they're drifting off to sleep. Psychology professor Dr. Richard Wiseman agrees. He believes napping at work is a great way to increase productivity, creativity, and worker focus.

If you're concerned that taking a nap will create the impression that you're a slacker, just take a look at legendary people who swore by power naps:

⊦ Winston Churchill used to plan his strategic meetings around his naptime. A NYTimes.com article in January 2000 quotes him as saying, "You must sleep sometime between lunch and dinner, and no halfway measures. Take off your clothes and get into bed. That's what I always do. Don't think you will be doing less work because you sleep during the day. That's a foolish notion held by people who have no imaginations. You will be able to accomplish more. You get two days in one—well, at least one and a half."

⊦ American Presidents Ronald Reagan and Bill Clinton were famous for their naps. And John F. Kennedy was often seen taking 15-minute naps by leaning back and putting his forearm over his face.

⊦ Albert Einstein used to take afternoon naps to recuperate and was quoted many times on his thoughts about how naps increased his productivity, creativity, and intuition.

⊦ Brahms napped at the piano while he composed his famous lullaby.

⊦ Thomas Edison, the inventor of the electric light, used to take frequent naps during the day instead of sleeping at night.

Dr. David Dinges, a sleep researcher at the University of Pennsylvania, is a strong advocate of prophylactic napping, taking what he and others call a "power nap" during the day to head off the cumulative effects of sleep loss. He explained in a research article (*www.ncbi.nlm.nih.gov*) that the brain "sort of sputters" when it's deprived of sufficient sleep, causing slips in performance and attentiveness.

Dr. James Maas, a Cornell University psychologist and author of *Power Sleep*, agrees in this book, pointing out that naps "greatly strengthen the ability to pay close attention to details and to make critical decisions."

We may be facing the day when your place of work actually encourages you—as my kindergarten teacher did—to "put your head down on your desks and rest a while." When you see the boost in creativity and productivity—*and* your intuition—you'll be glad you did!

Put Your Intuition to Work Tip

Get away from your office and take a brief creativity break. It's one of the quickest ways to make a decision or come up with a solution to a thorny problem.

{ }

| | | Put Your Intuition to Work Technique | | |
What's Your Ideal Outcome?

Intuition is the supra-logic that cuts out all the routine processes of thought and leaps straight from the problem to the answer.

–Robert Graves, Irish novelist

Whether you're trying to decide on a new hire or the best plan for a corporate merger, your intuition can guide you.

What's your ideal outcome?

Example: My perfect candidate for the floor manager position would be:

A great team leader.	Detail oriented.
An exemplary communicator.	Comfortable with diversity.

Focus within. Gather the list of resumes or candidate names you're considering for this position. Shut the door to your office and hold your calls. Close your eyes, take a deep breath and center yourself. "Who is the right person to hire?"

Intuition answers by one or all of the following:

꜀ The name of the ideal hire leaps to mind.

꜀ You have a strong positive feeling about one of the applicants.

꜀ You have a physical sensation such as a rush of energy that indicates a positive response.

꜀ You simply *know* the answer.

Chapter 10 | The Power of Enthusiasm

Enthusiasm is the yeast that makes your hopes shine to the stars. Enthusiasm is the sparkle in your eyes, the swing in your gait. The grip of your hand, the irresistible surge of will and energy to execute your ideas.

—Henry Ford, founder of The Ford Motor Company

Michelle is one of my clients who clearly loves her work as a social media consultant. She's one of those enviable folks who has potential customers flocking to seminars and paying her large retainers to work with them and their companies. She tells me that intuition is a large part of her business success:

I pay close attention to what I feel excited about. I believe that a feeling of fun, enthusiasm, and joy is a message from my intuition about what to move toward. These feelings guide me to my next steps in both my business and life in general. I guess I could say they act like my intuitive business plan!

My intuition tells me things before my head figures it out. I ask my intuition questions such as, "What do I need to know about this potential business opportunity?" or "What does this client need in order to grow their business?" In addition to getting "feel-ings" about things, the answers come in short phrases that pop into my head.

I asked Michelle to elaborate, and she did:

I have an intuitive process when I'm making a business decision. I sit in a comfortable chair in my office and shut off my phone and e-mail. I use an old-fashioned yellow lined pad of paper and a pen for this exercise. At the top of the page, I write something about the business direction or choice I'm seeking guidance about. I close my eyes and simply state in my mind, "I need information."

Short phrases and fragments of information come to me. It feels different in some way than just my everyday inner dialogue. It might say "Try this" or "Beware of that." If I'm lucky, I get a whole social media campaign idea that downloads in one fell swoop. I can tell when it's a winner because I feel excited about it. The enthusiasm is my confirmation that I have an idea that will be a big success.

I'll give you an example. I had a corporate client that had a reputation as being a bit boring and staid. They needed to spice up their image a bit to appeal to a younger audience. Most of the social media messaging was coming from the CEO who generally posted things about statistics and earnings, etc. While doing the intuitive exercise I just described, I heard the words "Try a cartoon." What most people didn't know about this CEO was that he rode a Harley. The image I received was a caricature of the man on his motorcycle. I thought we could use it to replace his dull, standard photo on all his social media profiles. I felt that hit of excitement and knew I had a winner if only I could convince him. Much to my surprise, he loved it! Once we implemented it, his fan base and those of the other company executives skyrocketed.

What Feels Enticing?

The word *enthusiasm* comes from the Greek root *entheos,* meaning "God within" or "guidance within." You might call it enthusiasm, passion, interest, zest, vitality, or energy. However, as Michelle suggests, it provides an important clue whenever you're trying to make a decision. Jonas Salk, the inventor of the polio vaccine, may have been thinking about this when he said, according to BrainyQuote.com, "It's always with excitement that I wake up in the morning wondering what my intuition will toss up to me, like gifts from the sea. I work with it and rely on it. It's my partner."

It makes sense on some very logical level to pay attention to your enthusiasm, whether you're thinking about a career change, a hiring decision, or working with a certain client. Simply put, if something feels exciting or has a lot of vitality, it's an indication from your intuition about the direction to follow. Conversely, if a decision makes you feel drained, bored, or enervated, it's a strong signal to move away from that choice.

This sense of enthusiasm is most critically important when you're contemplating a change in career direction. Brian had been an agent in the life insurance field for more than 30 years. He consistently won awards from his company as one of the top-10 agents in the country. He was making a great living, he had the acknowledgment of his company and respect from peers, and his clients loved him.

Life was bliss, right? That's what Brian kept telling himself every morning when he got out of bed. He says, "I should be happy. I've achieved everything I ever wanted. What more is there?" Yet he couldn't shake the feeling of malaise he had begun to experience almost a year earlier at an awards ceremony honoring him for his achievements. "Here I was at the top of my game and I felt like s---. It got so bad, I even talked to my doctor about getting on antidepressants. And I'm the quintessential optimist! Everyone who knows me knows I'm up, positive, cheerful. The glass is always half full for me."

He remembers picking up the book *Managing Upside Down* by Tom Chappell, the CEO and co-founder of Tom's of Maine. A phrase leapt out at him. It was one of the seven "intentions" mentioned by Chapell to help managers achieve far-reaching results. "Envision your destiny! Imagine your future with your head and your heart," it read.

Brian said he had never before thought of himself as a co-creator of his life. "I had a job. I was good at it. I made decent money. I provided a high-quality service. That was who I was. I had followed the path of least resistance in my life and had the good fortune to have it work out. Now it wasn't. Life just felt boring. I'd lost my passion. That phrase encouraging me to 'envision my destiny' got me fired up! I began to examine my values with particular attention to where I felt a glimmer of enthusiasm and vitality."

Brian decided to accelerate the process of self-discovery by working with me to help him follow his intuition to a new career. As he diligently worked on the idea of a new vocation, he saw he could integrate many of the aptitudes he possessed that had made him successful, and reconfigure them in a new career.

I asked him to put aside for now the question of how he would implement his choices. That would come later. I explained that often people put the cart before the horse; they try to decide how they're going to achieve something before fully deciding what they really want. By doing that, they usually manage to talk themselves out of whatever initially excited them. The phrase, "that's just not realistic" has doomed many an intuitive impulse right from the start.

Answers From Your Vitality Meter

Following is a list of questions I asked him to think about as he reflected on various vocational options. You may want to get your notebook and write down the answers for yourself. This technique works for a variety of issues. It doesn't need to be a career-focused concern. Try it out when you're making your next hiring decision, when contemplating working with a new client or when you're trying to figure out how to approach a potentially difficult conversation.

Think of the options you have before you. List at least six in your notebook.

Which one(s) are you drawn to?

Is there one that leaps to your attention?

Do one or more of the choices feel draining or enervating?

Do you feel a sense of excitement about one over the others?

Is there a visceral response you receive about pursuing this course of action? (A physical sensation is one of the ways that intuition communicates.)

What action do you feel most enthusiastic about? That's the right direction to follow.

Brian listed his options as follows. I included his notes in parentheses to give you an idea about how this works.

1. Stay in my present job until I retire. (No energy there. Makes me want to go to sleep.)

2. Take some courses at the local college in psychology or a similar topic. (That reaches about a 4 on the vitality meter. Not high enough!)

3. Take a year off and hope that at the end of that time I'll have it all figured out. (That makes me much too nervous and I'd drive my wife crazy.)

4. Work part-time at my current job and explore options around starting a sales training business. (That one gets the vitality meter hitting high marks!)

5. Investigate becoming a life coach and help other business people explore career change. (That scores a 5 on a scale of 1 to 10. I'm concerned that talking with people about problems isn't my forte. I'm also not very patient.)

6. Look into joining the National Speakers Association and/or Toastmasters to uncover ways to make a living as a trainer/consultant in sales. (Definitely excited about this.)

After going over this list and discussing it with his wife and several trusted friends, Brian decided his vitality meter was pointing him in the direction of creating his own sales training business. Numbers 4 and 6 were the indicators for him. The thought of completely leaving his current job didn't feel right. Fortunately he was able to negotiate staying in insurance sales part-time. That gave him both an income cushion and some structure that felt comfortable to him.

I received an e-mail from Brian several months after our initial session. It read, "The vitality meter was right! I have four contracts for sales training this month alone. It's amazing how when you're on the right track, business just comes to you!"

To figure out what your vitality meter is indicating to you, set aside time when you won't be disturbed. Find a quiet, comfortable place and relax. Stay quiet and settle into a mind frame of calmness and peace. Give yourself permission to take 10 to 20 minutes for this exercise. When your mind is still, there are a number of questions you could ask:

What am I yearning for?

What excites me right now?

What's my right next step?

Or simply make up questions of your own. Listen. Allow your intuition—the whispers in your mind, the deep inner knowing in your heart, the wisdom within—to guide you. Allow the answers to bubble to the surface. You may have a flash of insight, or a nagging feeling that takes longer to explain. Repeat the process again and again. Here are more questions to ask:

What makes me happy? What fills me with passion? What projects do I look forward to? Which activities make it easy to jump out of bed in the morning?

What job would incorporate my passion with service to others? Can I find a role that will help those around me fulfill their goals?

Have opportunities appeared that help me on my journey towards change?

Will my new path allow me to use my unique abilities? Does it honor the individual that I am? Do I feel excited about it?

Keep Going

You're unique. Listen to your heart and participate in your own life. No one else can fill the role that's been intended for you. When you're moving in the right direction, every moment will feel so full that you won't believe how long it took you to make a change. It does take courage! The confidence will come as you begin to take action.

So start your business, write your book, take time to travel or begin one of myriad things that you want to pursue and the whole world will begin to open up to you. Keep walking toward what truly makes you vital and happy. That's putting your intuition to work for you!

Put Your Intuition to Work Tip
When you're trying to make a decision, write down your options. As you review the list, notice how you respond. Which option scores the highest on your "inner vitality meter"? The guidepost you can trust is the sense of openness, ease, and curiosity.

| | | Put Your Intuition to Work Technique | | |
Small Steps Lead to Big Strides

We go the direction we face, and we face the direction we think.
—Jim Rohn, author, entrepreneur, and motivational speaker

When you're clear you're headed in the wrong direction, the obvious question is "What's next?" If you're like most people, you don't want to take any action until you have a crystal-clear goal. Many of my clients call me when they're in that particular limbo state. It's uncomfortable to feel stuck.

I believe that intuition not only tells you when you're on the wrong path, it also provides the clues to get you back on track.

What are some things you enjoy? Make a plan to do at least one of those things every day. Think of those small pleasures as part of the direction your intuition is providing to get you back on the right track. This may not make logical sense to you, but do it anyway. What have you got to lose, besides a few moments away from feeling bad? Begin to notice what you feel excited about. That's a clue about what to pursue.

Focus on where you want to go. If a project has failed, you're out of work, or you're experiencing some other form of setback it's all too easy to rehash the past. Most of the time, that's wasted energy and will only serve to keep you feeling down. If you don't have a clear goal, focus on what you know. These might be objectives like "I want a position where I'll have autonomy," "I want to feel excited about my work again," or "I want some clear direction." When you can state what you want, your intuition will begin to provide guidance to get you there.

Take small steps every day. If you're in a major life transition, you may be feeling overwhelmed and lacking direction.

Instead of trying to figure out the next big goal or plan, take smaller steps. Make your first goal figuring out what you want to do. What might that look like on a day-to-day basis?

- Take a class in a subject that interests you.
- Read a book on the subject.
- Talk to someone who has the type of job you're curious about.
- Speak with someone who has had a similar problem to the one you're facing.
- Hang out with people who are encouraging and upbeat.
- Go on a retreat (and take your intuition journal!).
- Have lunch with someone whose advice you value.
- Volunteer doing something you enjoy.
- Join a group or association that relates to your area of interest.

What are you doing that's on the mark? What are you doing that feels off the mark? If one way doesn't work for you, be ready to go to another. Many times, the road to success is found by taking a detour.

Cultivate the attitude of having had a wish fulfilled. Success is waiting for you. Use the power of visualization and affirmation to vividly imagine, sense and feel the life you want to live.

I love this quote by Michael Angier that I found on GreatThoughtsTreasury.com: "A successful day: to learn something new; to laugh at least 10 times; to lift someone up; to make progress on a worthy goal; to practice peace and patience; to do something nice for yourself and another; to appreciate and be grateful for all your blessings."

Chapter 11 | Is It Fear or Intuition?

It's within you: the answers you seek, the direction you want, and the power to be whoever you want to be. Your dreams are not yours by mere whim. They've been meticulously matched to the gifts you're now developing. Designed to lure you within, where your true power lies, and then out into the world, beyond imagined limitations and fears. Trust yourself. Listen to your heart. You have the right stuff, you know what to do, and it can all be yours.

—Mike Dooley, author of *Notes From the Universe*

Anne's boss, Mitch, waved to her as she was heading out the door one Friday afternoon, adding, "Hey! Come in to see me Monday morning. I have something I want to discuss with you!" She waved back and said she'd be there. She walked to her car and turned the ignition, and anxiety began to set in. What did he want to talk to her about? Had she made a mistake? If he was going to fire her, he'd probably do that on a Friday, not a Monday morning, right? Perhaps it was the pitch she was working on for a new business proposal. She had given it to him earlier in the week. Maybe he didn't like it? Her mind was reeling and she spent the weekend worried about the meeting.

On Monday morning, Mitch greeted Anne warmly as she walked into his office. He spoke to her animatedly about an opportunity he had for her to lead a new business division the company was starting soon. They spoke about the position for about 30 minutes before he had to leave for another meeting. He answered all her questions and asked if she'd be interested. They agreed she could take a day to sleep on it and get back to him on Tuesday.

After leaving Mitch's office Anne's mind filled with fear. She says:

Mitch obviously feels strongly that I'm the right person for the promotion. But, can I do it? There would be a lot of pressure to perform, an expectation that I could get the division up and profitable within a short period of time. Would I have the right staff? Did I have the right skills? The more I thought about it, the more I became convinced that my intuition was telling me this wouldn't be a good decision. I couldn't seem to differentiate my fear, negative self-talk, and intuition. They were all jumbled together. That's when I decided to call for an intuitive consultation.

Fear Is Normal When You Move Out of Your Comfort Zone

Anne's concern is a very common one. How do you determine if it's a self-imposed fear or if it's your intuition warning you away from something? It's the most frequently asked question I get when I'm doing training on how to develop your intuition for business audiences. Here's the process I use to differentiate the two.

What's Making You Feel Afraid?

Grab a notebook and pen and begin writing. Don't think about this too much. This is more of a freeflowing, get-it-on-the-page exercise. You might think about this as your worst-case scenario page. Putting those things down in black and white can help you evaluate them both logically and intuitively.

What Are Your Typical Fears?

I could alternately title this section "Know Thyself." Think about a big decision you've made in the past. It could be a decision to move, change jobs, get married (or divorced), or shift your major in college. On a separate piece of paper, make another list and answer a series of questions. How did you make the decision? What were some fears or concerns you had? Are they some of the same ones you're experiencing now? What did you learn about making your decision? Were you happy with the outcome of that choice? What worked for you in this decision-making process? What do you wish you had done differently?

Evaluate Your Lists

You will notice that many of the things you've written down will be future oriented. "What if this happens?" "What if that happens?" Some of the possible outcomes are going to be about issues you have no realistic way of knowing. (Even I don't have that crystal ball!) Once you see those fears and questions on paper, you have some options. Is there more information you can gather to put your concerns to rest, or at least feel a little less anxious? If not, can you live with some of the possible outcomes or reduce their impact?

As we talked, Anne became aware that her decision-making style was to always imagine the worst possible outcome first. She goes through all the various awful things that might occur and then convinces herself that they'll probably happen. She then becomes paralyzed by fear and indecision. Talking through them and writing them down were helpful. She could then see them more clearly for what they were.

She also realized there was some benefit for her in doing this. Thinking about and recognizing what could happen better prepared her for those possibilities. She also understood that if she simply assumed all the fears were true, they prevented her from making decisions that could be beneficial to her both professionally and personally in the future.

In Anne's case, many of her concerns were legitimate. Would she have enough staff and resources? Would there be definable and realistic goals for the new division? What was her job description and did she have the right skill set? As she wrote these down, she realized that she actually didn't have the answers to these things at the moment and needed to have a more detailed discussion with Mitch. She told me that she was asking the questions in her own mind and coming up with a negative answer for each one. That was what was causing her to feel fear.

She set up a meeting with Mitch the following day with a list of issues to discuss. They were able to go through each one and come up with an action plan that satisfied both of them. The fears dissipated and were replaced with a little more confidence. She reported back to me later that she accepted the position and that it was going well. She was very glad to have not given in to her fear over her intuition.

What Accurate Information Looks and Feels Like

You feel open and expansive.

It feels right in your body—usually your gut and/or chest.

The information elicits neutral to mild interest/curiosity.

Any inner messages you receive are compassionate, neutral, or kind.

Intuition conveys a detached message: "Yes. This is the right direction."

You may feel that you're out of your comfort zone, but still feel guided to move ahead with the decision.

When It's Fear, Not Intuition

You feel overwrought, too-excited, and emotional.

You're hearing an inner voice that is criticizing or demeaning: "You're not good enough!" "You'll fail at that."

You whipsaw back and forth between a yes and no decision, and don't come to some gut or heart-centered place.

The decision reflects poor self-esteem or other psychological wound.

You feel very off balance. You're paralyzed or stuck in inaction.

When It's Intuition, Not Fear

Let me give you another example from my own life. Whenever a new book is published, there are two main considerations. The first, obviously, is to write it well so people will want to read it. The second is to work hard at marketing to make more readers aware of the book.

Shortly after the first edition of *Divine Intuition* was published, I received a call from a journalist writing for a top-tier magazine. She was doing an article on intuition and wanted to interview me. Wow! This was a great opportunity! My book would be mentioned in an article seen by hundreds of thousands of people. My publisher would be thrilled. I could see "best-seller" written on the cover of future editions.

The problem was that every time I went to pick up the phone to set up the interview, I couldn't do it. My stomach clenched. My heart sank. I felt discouraged. I sat down and meditated and asked, "Should I do this interview?" The answer kept coming back through both body sensation and words: no. My head was arguing furiously with this answer. My logical mind wanted desperately to do it for all the aforementioned reasons.

I checked in with myself. Was I fearful of anything she might ask? Was I engaging in unreasonable, negative self-talk? Was this interview simply out of my comfort zone and making me uncomfortable? The answers kept coming back no. I figured that more information might be helpful.

I decided to call the reporter back and simply ask for more information about the focus and tone of the article. She replied that it was an instructive, upbeat piece about the pros and cons of intuition. In the midst of the brief conversation I was overcome with a feeling of dread and felt very strongly I shouldn't do it. I finally ended the conversation saying, "My intuition is telling me I'm not the right person to interview for this article." She tried to convince me otherwise and I just repeated that sentence, and we hung up.

I would have to wait a few months before the article appeared in print. The headline was something like "Skeptics Say Intuition Is Nonsense." It went on to paint a picture of anyone who uses intuition as engaged in New Age "woo-woo." Several of my professional colleagues had been featured, and their comments and expertise had been reduced to a few statements that seemed designed to make them appear off-balance and nutty. Suffice to say that the article was not what I would have expected from this publication and I was very glad my intuition had alerted me.

Caution Messages

What about the situations where intuition is definitely indicating a warning through giving you messages of outright fear? Gavin de Becker is a danger analyst and wrote the seminal book on this topic, *The Gift of Fear*. He's quoted in a 2010 PsychologyToday.com article as saying, "We get a signal prior to violence," de Becker says. "There are pre-incident indicators. Things that happen before violence occurs."

Women especially override their intuition because of a strong cultural leaning to "be polite." De Becker gives the example of a woman waiting for an elevator. As the doors open, a man steps in with her. Our intuitive brains have a way of quickly assessing a situation without conscious input. It may be the way the man was dressed, his body posture, the way he greeted (or didn't greet) her. It could be a whole host of sub-conscious clues she is picking up. Whatever the reasons, our hypothetical woman immediately senses a dangerous situation. Not wanting to appear rude, she doesn't get off the elevator. She realizes only too late that he has a gun and is planning to use it.

De Becker says that "eerie feelings" are exactly what he wants women to pay attention to. In the same PsychologyToday.com article he states, "We're trying to analyze the warning signs." he says. What he wants people to understand is "[t]he feeling of the warning sign. All the other stuff is our explanation for the feeling. Why it was this, why it was that. The feeling itself *is* the warning sign."

In *The Gift of Fear* de Becker states that a great deal of threat management depends on our intuitive awareness. It's that sense of danger that causes the hair on the back of your neck to stand on end or spikes a sensation of fear in some part of your brain. So the next time you walk through the door to your office building that was unlocked and should have been locked, pay attention. Or when the offer for a job interview takes you to an unknown location late at night and it makes you uncomfortable, listen to that inner wisdom. After all, as de Becker states, your life could depend on trusting those instincts.

Put Your Intuition to Work Tip
Think back to a time when you made a significant life decision. What were some of the factors that went into making a successful choice? Even if it moved you out of your comfort zone, how did you know the decision was right for you?

{ }

Chapter 12 | Your Higher Power at Work
Listen to me; keep silent, and I will teach you wisdom.

—Job 33:33

Intuition is a ready source of direction—a compass of the soul—available to all of us. It's an invisible intelligence that animates our world and provides wisdom to guide our lives. When we follow its wisdom, it invariably leads us to success and happiness in both our personal and business lives.

I've often joked that it would be wonderful to arrive in this world with an instruction manual that gives us step-by-step directions for living a full and happy life, as well as for succeeding in business. Through the years, I've come to understand that we do, in fact, receive this guidance. We're hard-wired for this source of wisdom through our intuition.

Fortunately, we all have the ability to tap into this power. We are all capable of developing it for practical use in everyday life, as well as for discovering and achieving life goals. Many people think of it as the domain of a gifted few, even though intuition is now recognized not as a rare, accidental talent, but as a natural skill that all of us can cultivate.

Learning to trust your gut at work is much more than simply paying attention to your hunches. It involves looking within for the answers, living life with courage, faith, patience, and trust. It also involves connecting with your Spirit through daily practice and taking action on the wisdom you receive.

In a recent *Today* show poll of 1,500 people, 68 percent of the respondents stated that they believe that God exists. "A majority of those surveyed believe the power of prayer is real, and 76 percent say it can heal. Roughly half (54 percent) said they pray regularly, while little over a quarter (27 percent) said they pray only in a time of need." (You can view the entire survey at http://tinyurl.com/Today-comPrayer.)

The Still, Quiet Inner Voice

My personal belief is that there is a wise, loving, and creative intelligence that we are all part of. It guides our thoughts, provides inspired ideas, and connects us to each other. Many of the people I interviewed for this book felt strongly that their intuition comes from a spiritual source. They argued that hunches and instinct weren't simply pattern recognition or awareness of subconscious information. They alluded to intuition more as a sixth sense or the proverbial "still, quiet inner voice" that unites them to their higher self.

Each person had a unique way of describing this "invisible intelligence." They called it by different names: God, wisdom within, universal intelligence, higher self or simply a higher consciousness.

Prayer is the primary way we talk to God about our concerns. I believe that intuition is one of the ways God answers. A thought may pop into your mind. The person with the answer to your problem may coincidentally walk into your office. Or, you may act on an impulse to turn on the radio at just the right time to hear someone provide an insight you need. Asking for guidance through prayer is something easily done at work. "Dr. T," MD, is a board-certified obstetrician/gynecologist practicing in California. She has an absolute conviction that prayer works. She credits answers to prayers with saving the lives of patients. She treats many high-risk patients and frequently has to make critical and immediate life-or-death decisions. Those intuitive answers come through in a unique way for Dr. T. She hears it as a distinct and commanding deep male voice that seems to come from behind her right shoulder.

Dr. T says:

I was recently performing a caesarean section on a normal, healthy pregnant woman, who was having her fourth child. It was a routine case and was proceeding normally. All of a sudden I heard a command stating "Get blood now!" This made no logical sense. There was nothing at all to indicate that the patient would have any problem. However, I've learned that whenever this inner voice communicates it is unerringly accurate. I honestly don't know how a doctor can function without this guidance.

I turned to the OR nurse and asked her to "type and cross" four units of packed red blood cells, and to thaw some fresh frozen plasma. The nurses I work with understand and respect the intuitive manner of many of my decisions (and because of this, many of these nurses are also my patients). She didn't question me, and immediately called the blood bank. The anesthesiologist, on the other hand, loudly objected and stated, "There's nothing wrong here, this patient is rock stable and no blood is needed. What is wrong with you?" He commanded the nurse not *to order the blood.*

Fortunately, the nurse ignored him, and ordered the blood products. Approximately 15 minutes later, the patient began to massively hemmorrhage. Blood was pouring out of her, all over me and onto the floor. Mercifully, the crossmatching process was almost complete and the patient was able to rapidly receive multiple units of blood and fresh frozen plasma in order to save her life.

Emergency Intuition

Dr. T described two other occasions when this inner voice positively impacted the lives of others:

I was called to the emergency room to consult on a patient who was 28 weeks pregnant. She was spiking extremely high fevers and had violent shaking chills. The patient had been thoroughly evaluated by the emergency room physician and also by an internist and an infection disease specialist. They were unable to come up with a diagnosis and were at a loss as to how to treat her. As I walked into her room, the voice calmly stated, "She has malaria." Malaria had been "eradicated" in the United States in 1951, and the few sporadic cases that had occurred since then were mostly in the southern states. Rapid and accurate diagnosis of malaria is essential in order to appropriately treat the patient, and to prevent the further spread of the infection.

When I told the ER physician that the patient had malaria, he began laughing hysterically and informed me that only a gynecologist could be stupid enough to come up with a diagnosis like that. Fortunately, he ran the blood work and the patient was rapidly and appropriately diagnosed and treated for malaria.

Dr. T's next experience involved a 16-year-old girl who recently had undergone surgery to have a large ovarian tumor removed:

The patient did well after surgery and went home on postoperative day four. A few days later, the patient presented to the emergency room, complaining of severe abdominal pain. The emergency room physician did a gigantic work-up with multiple tests, could find "nothing wrong" with her, and sent her home on antibiotics. On each of the next two days, the patient again came to the ER with severe pain and was again sent home. On the fourth day, the patient came in to my office and was seen by my nurse practitioner who then called me. I instructed the nurse practitioner to send the patient to the hospital for a "direct admit." My plan was to keep the patient in the hospital until she had an accurate diagnosis, treatment, and recovery.

Upon entering this young girl's room, I heard the voice state, "She has necrotizing fasciitis." Necrotizing fasciitis, commonly known as "flesh-eating bacteria," is a rare, life-threatening infection resulting in the necrosis (dying) of the skin, subcutaneous tissue, and fascia. 73 percent of the people with NF die from it. Because of this disease's rapid progression, it is important to diagnose and treat NF quickly to avoid death.

I had never seen a case of NF and did not know any physician who ever had. It is so rare that it only occurs in 1 in 1,250,000 children.

*I immediately called in the infectious disease physician to see
the patient. I told him that I thought my patient had necrotizing
fasciitis (NF). He reviewed the patient's chart and carefully
examined her. He then told me that there was 'no need' for me to
be "a histrionic female physician." He stated that my patient had a
"simple staph infection" and that if she didn't improve in three to
four days, he would then change her antibiotics. I felt sick (frantic),
and I knew that the patient would quickly die without rapid
treatment. I called the hospitalist surgeon and told her that I knew
the patient had NF and asked her to come right away.*

*She examined the patient, who by now had big, black, blisters
on her abdomen, and within 15 minutes the surgeon had the
patient in the operating room. The patient had to have extensive
debridement of her entire abdominal wall. It took four months of
care in the intensive care unit, multiple surgeries, multiple blood
transfusions and high powered antibiotics to keep this young girl
alive. Fortunately, she recovered.*

Dr. T attributes much of her inner wisdom to prayer and
believes it opens her to the guidance she receives. Many people
also report feeling a strong connection between their spirituality and intuition. They're not willing to simply chalk up their
strong intuitions to subconscious or prior knowledge coming
to the surface just when they need it.

How to Connect With This Wisdom

May McCarthy is another person who connects to this
wisdom in a unique way. She has helped to start and grow six
successful companies over her 32-year career, with the largest
growing to more than $100 million in annual sales. She attri-
butes her success to the daily practice that she describes in her
book, *The Path to Wealth: Seven Spiritual Steps for Financial
Abundance.*

Now a speaker and angel investor, she describes how
she brought into her business a valued advisor which she

affectionately calls the chief spiritual officer, or CSO for short. She chose this name for the all-knowing, universal power that some may call Infinite Intelligence, God, Spirit, Truth, or The Universe.

May says:

I surround myself with other C-suite executives whose advice I value. This includes my chief financial officer, my chief information officer, and my chief operating officer. I decided my chief spiritual officer would have the most valuable advice for me in all areas of my business, and I placed it at the top of my organizational chart and meet with it every day.

Every successful business leader knows that a daily planning session and goal review with top management is vital to a vibrant and profitable company. I schedule my meetings with my CSO first thing every morning. I have a specific format of seven steps. This is what it looks like: [See page 108]

May explains that the intuitive leads, hunches, and signs from her CSO may come in flashes, an urge to do something, a book or article she feels drawn to read, or an inner voice. Flashes show up as a vision, thought, or idea. They seem to pop up out of nowhere without warning. "A hunch is usually felt in the center of my body and brews there for a bit of time with emotion," May says.

She recalls having a strong urge to drive to a somewhat distant supermarket at 9:00 one evening. There wasn't anything out of the ordinary that she needed, but she isn't one to dispute her CSO hunches. As she was walking into the market, she ran into a potential client who was walking out. During their conversation, the potential client invited May to make a sales presentation to their company that resulted in a new order valued at more than $400,000.

May points out that there are clear roles and responsibilities in your partnership with your CSO. Your job is to define

Date: _____

The CSO and I attended the meeting.

Step 1: Read something spiritual and uplifting to get into a receptive mood.

Step 2: Write out gratitude statements in a letter to the CSO. I include those things that I'm grateful for and those that I want, as though they were already manifested in my life. (I use a notebook for this daily letter.)

Step 3: I speak with emotion as I read the letter out loud.

Step 4: I imagine, think about, feel grateful for all that I've listed as my desires. I do this as if they've already manifested. I focus on the following: What does it feel like to have them now? What does my life look like with these things or experiences?

During this step, I may feel some intuitive guidance from my CSO. If I receive this information at this time, I write it down and take action on it after our meeting. If I don't hear or receive insight at that time, that's okay. I know it will come later and I'll follow it then.

The next three steps occur later in the day.

Step 5: I watch every moment of the day for a sign or some intuitive direction to take the next step towards my desired goal. I follow any leads, flashes, and hunches that I've received and write them down in my notebook.

Step 6: I celebrate and express gratitude when something good happens that's related to what I want. I might call or text a friend or colleague to acknowledge this occasion. I note any demonstrations in my notebook.

Step 7: As I prepare for bed at night, I say out loud my gratitude statements for anything that happened that day. I also thank my CSO. In addition, I commit to forgiving anyone, myself included, for anything that's occurred, past or present, that I need to clear out of my life.

what you want with gratitude as though you've already received it. The CSO's job is to create the path to get to your goal and give you one step to take at a time. You either take the step or ask for another lead or sign from your CSO. Eventually, you reach your goals. It's that simple.

Put Your Intuition to Work Tip

Intuition works best when you're calm. Think about the outcome you want and then try things like going for a short walk, meditating for a few minutes or pushing away from your desk or simply taking a few deep centering breaths. What does your intuition communicate now?

Chapter 13 | Learn to Thrive Through Change

When written in Chinese, the word "crisis" is composed of two characters. One represents danger and the other represents opportunity.

—John F. Kennedy

We've all experienced it. Despite your best intentions, life becomes over-the-top stressful. It may have happened after you carefully planned the presentation to your biggest client. Everything was perfect. But as you're heading to the big meeting, you receive a call that your husband was in a car accident and is on the way to the hospital.

Or, everything is in place for the promotion of your firm's new product. It's been years in the making, press releases have gone out, the media is interested, your staff is prepped, orders are beginning to pour in. And you discover an error in the manufacturing of your product. That's what happened to Steve, the CEO of a major personal care products firm.

We had completed all the prototypes for our product and it worked perfectly. It was a cutting-edge creation. There was nothing out there in the market like it. The first month it was on the shelves, we were getting glowing reports from our customers and reviewers. Then, inexplicably, something changed. We began to get a large number of calls to our customer service lines saying our product was defective.

I called the product development team into my office for an emergency meeting. Unfortunately, they were as baffled as I was. They were looking to me for the answer, and honestly, I felt totally overwhelmed and didn't know where to begin. I talked to my public relations director and we crafted a message to give to the press who were beginning to catch on to our problem. Frankly, as the day progressed, I felt I was becoming more and more ineffective, and I still didn't have a clue to what the answer was.

Finally, I did what I should have done earlier. I closed the door, asked my assistant to put my calls on hold, sat down, and put my feet up on my desk. I had taken a class on intuition several years prior to this. Since then, my trust in my intuition had gotten stronger, and I relied on it more and more, especially when I was in a personal or business crisis. Clearly I needed it today.

I'm a spiritual man, not religious. I know that when I'm overwhelmed, I just need to quiet myself and pray. The great hotelier, Conrad Hilton said, "Intuition can be a form of answered prayer. You do the best you can—thinking, figuring, planning— and then you pray." I take that to heart. The answers are always there inside of me. They come to me through my intuition. I also know I can crowd them out by being anxious. I've used meditation and dream journaling as tools to help me access this inner wisdom, but I believe the scriptural admonition to "pray without ceasing" is a directive to always be mindful that the Resource is always there.

I decided to simply let all the emotions I felt flow over me. The panic, confusion, fear, and anxiety just bubbled to the surface. I tried not to resist anything. When I finally felt that my insides were quiet enough, I posed a simple question: "What is the best course of action for me to take right now?"

I receive much of my intuition visually, through images and symbolic pictures. As soon as I asked the question, a short mental slide show began to form inside my mind. First I saw the number 2. Then I saw an image of someone holding two of our products. After that I noticed that the two products looked different. At first I couldn't figure it out.

The three "slides" kept repeating themselves so I asked a different question: "What's the next step?" This time I didn't see the information. I heard it. It was simply the phrase "Talk to Joe." I know a number of Joes, but the one that came immediately to my mind was our contact person at the factory in China where our products are made.

It turns out that my intuition was dead on. I called Joe and learned they had duplicated the mold of our product without informing us. He figured he was doing us a favor in order to keep up with demand. Unfortunately, the specs on the second mold were microscopically off, but enough to result in a defective product.

I won't bore you with more details other than to say after a difficult few months, we came out okay and the product has gone on to become very successful. I thank God for my intuition. Without it, I don't know where we'd be.

Freeze-Frame It

The HeartMath Institute in Boulder Creek, California, has a wonderful technique they call "Freeze-Framing." I have found it very helpful to use when I'm in situations like Robert describes in the previous section—especially when my anxiety threatens to block out all insightful intuitive messages.

Doc Childre is the founder of the program and author of the book *The HeartMath Solution.* He's quoted on the Macquarie Institute Website explaining:

> When we're internally self-managed—feeling balanced, in control, and powerful—we make our greatest contribution. We act, not react. We think creatively. We communicate clearly. We manage well under pressure. We make good decisions. Our most inspiring leadership qualities emerge. When dozens, hundreds, thousands of employees work in that zone of peak performance, so does the organization.

If you're wondering how to use this information next time you're in a crisis or simply feeling anxious, try the following technique.

Recognize the stressful feeling and Freeze-Frame it. In other words, take time out. For example, see your problem as a still picture, not a movie. Stop the inner conversation you're having about the situation.

Make a sincere effort to shift your focus away from your racing mind or disturbed emotions, and concentrate on the area around your heart. Pretend you're breathing through your heart to help focus your energy. Keep your focus there for 10 seconds or more.

Bring to mind a positive feeling, or recall a time in your life when you were having fun. Hold that feeling for a few moments.

Now, using your intuition, ask your heart what would be a more efficient response to the situation—one that would minimize stress.

Listen to what your heart says in answer to your question. It's an effective way to put your reactive mind and emotions in check. It's like having an "in-house" source of wise solutions.

You may hear nothing, yet feel calmer. You may receive confirmation of something you already know, or you may experience a complete perspective shift, seeing the problem in a more balanced way. Although you may not have control over the event, you do have control over your perception of it and reaction to it.

The techniques taught at HeartMath are more extensive than the simple Freeze-Frame exercise. In fact they have several software programs and other leading-edge products. Their clinical studies have dramatically demonstrated the critical link among emotion, heart function, and cognitive performance. Their case studies have shown measurable improvements in leadership performance, sales effectiveness, customer service, staff retention, cost reductions, health, and overall performance through the use of their program.

Be Aware of *All* the Ways That Intuition Communicates

Ken is an electrical systems engineer employed by a company that manufactures and sells commercial satellites to companies like DirectTV, XM Satellite Radio, Sirius Satellite

Radio, and EchoStar. He's often in situations that require swift solutions in a chaotic and time-sensitive business. He describes a recent intuitive insight this way:

While working on the payload configuration of a communications satellite design, our customer suddenly changed the payload requirements, which meant the rewiring of 128 electrical connections. It takes three years to design, build, and test a custom satellite like this, so it's incredibly expensive to make these changes late in the game.

After about an hour of working on the problem, I told the project manager (my boss) that I had a solution that required the rewiring of just 16 connections, not 128. But I added that I knew deep inside there was another significantly better solution, and though I had no idea what it was, I knew I would find it.

My boss was already pleased with my 16-connection solution and didn't respond to my claim of an even better idea. However, later that day, I discovered I could solve the problem by breaking only one wire and inserting a relay in the middle. My new solution was presented to the customer, and he was extremely impressed. What impressed me, though, was the fact that my intuition had told me I had not yet solved a problem that everyone else felt was solved. I had been so certain about this, I told my boss about it before I had a clue as to what it was. I'm known as a problem solver and as a result my coworkers think I'm smart. I am smart—because I listen to my intuition and then take action.

How did Ken receive these intuitive impressions that saved his client tens of thousands of dollars? He says:

I believe the key is to simply be aware of what your mind and body is telling you. Sometimes I hear a faint voice, sometimes I just know something, and sometimes my gut tells me which direction to go. These are subtle signals that can easily be missed if you're not "listening." Being aware and grounded not only helps me tune into my intuition, it helps me live in the moment and fully experience life.

Your Guidance Is Always On

These stories are not unusual. They represent hundreds more I've heard just like them: tales of success in the face of crisis and chaos, stories with happy endings because their main characters listened to and heeded their intuition.

I like what Lissa Rankin, MD, wrote in her latest book, *The Anatomy of a Calling*, "Our culture tends to rush us through this space of uncertainty. We get impatient with ourselves and bully ourselves into doing something, while others try to hurry us along." It takes courage to trust this inner wisdom. It very often flies in the face of what others tell you to do or what your logical brain thinks is "right." Taking the time to reflect, to quiet your heart and mind enough to hear and feel the inner rhythm of life, is what intuition is all about. Trust the process of this inner wisdom. It's purpose is to guide you in all areas of your life.

How Do You Know You're on the Right Track?

Drs. Gay Hendricks and Kate Ludeman write in the book *The Corporate Mystic*, "The main reason intuition is so important is this: It is a clear sign that you are connecting with your inner spiritual guidance system. Intuition is a direct signal from your deepest self that you are navigating from your true center."

Our inner guidance system is really not all that complicated. Simply put, if you're feeling good and things are working out and you're in the flow of life, that's your intuition telling you to continue with whatever you're doing. Conversely, if things are stuck, are difficult, and you feel bad, your intuition is indicating a change of course is needed.

Need a checklist to know whether you're on the right track? Here it is:

ʕ I enjoy my work and life.

ʕ My connections with friends, colleagues, and family are strong.

ʕ I'm proud of my accomplishments.

ʕ I'm in the flow. Things happen fairly easily in my life without a lot of pushing and effort.

ʕ I help others through my product or my service, or simply by my example.

ʕ I feel confident.

ʕ I feel creative and challenged by my work.

ʕ I'm easily able to shift direction if something isn't working.

ʕ I listen to my intuition and follow its wisdom.

ʕ Doors of opportunity seem to open effortlessly.

ʕ People respond positively to me and my work.

ʕ I like what I do.

ʕ I wake up each day and look forward to it.

ʕ I feel motivated to do my best work.

ʕ I have a good work/life balance.

ʕ I feel positive about the future.

ʕ I sleep well at night.

ʕ I allow time for creative, personal, and/or spiritual interests.

If you agreed with five or more statements in the list, you're on the right path. You may not experience all of the above, all of the time. If you do, your intuition is giving you a pat on the back and encouragement to keep going!

If you're faced with a choice about a new project, job, assignment, or direction, put it to the intuition test. Here are two questions:

1. Is this something I want to do now?
2. Am I excited or energized by the thought of taking it on?

You'll know in your gut the right answer. It usually comes instantly without a lot of thought. If you feel you should do it or feel duty-bound to say yes, wait. Try this answer: "Let me think about this and get back to you." Then spend some time with any of the exercises you've learned in this book to determine what your intuition is telling you about this decision.

Remember: When you say no to what you don't want, you're allowing space in your life for something better.

Put Your Intuition to Work Tip
When you're in a chaotic situation, make a sincere effort to shift your focus away from your racing mind or anxiety. Concentrate on the area around your heart. While keeping your focus there, ask your intuition for a more efficient response to the situation.

Chapter 14 | What to Do When You Don't Know What to Do

Don't let the noise of other's opinions drown out your own inner voice. And most important, have the courage to follow your heart and intuition. They somehow already know what you truly want to become. Everything else is secondary.

—Steve Jobs, co-founder, Apple Computer

It happens to all of us: that painful moment you realize you're stuck in a rut. The job that once felt so stimulating is now boring. You've "been there, done that." It often comes on slowly. You just aren't that interested in spearheading the new company initiative. Or a new client approaches you with potential business, but you keep putting off the follow-up necessary to close the sale. You may even be out of work and unable to figure out what's next, and you're not interested in going back to the same career you had before.

You may feel depressed, a little scared, or anxious. Those are the hallmarks of your intuition giving you a gentle nudge and saying, in effect, "change is needed." Anytime you find yourself consistently bored, drained, or depleted, look at it as a wake-up call.

Your intuition is your inner compass. It delivers the message that you need to head in a new direction and shows you the best path to get there. However, sometimes it's hard to get started. Alexander Graham Bell, the inventor of the telephone, went through many transitions in his life. He said, "When one door closes, another opens: but we often look so long and so regretfully upon the closed door that we do not see the one which has opened for us."

Jerry came to see me as a client. He looked like the epitome of the successful business leader that he was. He told me that he had recently won the CFO (chief financial officer) of the Year Award. The company he worked for was growing by leaps and bounds. He made a very healthy income supplemented by yearly bonuses that allowed him to buy a vacation home in the past year.

The problem?

I'm in a rut. I have no time for my family. I don't have time for any creative pursuits. The company I work for is now so large, that I feel disconnected from both the employees and the larger vision of the organization. I went into this because I felt my skills were put to good use and I was offering a service I was proud of. Now my gut is telling me it's time to leave. I've always been goal-oriented. But I don't know what I want next. Is it crazy to think about leaving? I have the life most people dream of having and yet I'm not happy.

Jerry's transition to a new life didn't happen overnight. He ultimately made the decision to work for the company as a consultant instead of a full-time employee. This choice was initially met with a fair amount of resistance from both his family as well as the CEO that he reported to. Jerry says:

Even though I was scared, terrified at times, I had to stay true to myself. I felt like I was dying inside. In fact, I had several dreams where the message seemed to be that if I stayed at my company, I would get sick. At one point, that actually seemed like an honorable way to get out.

I needed to stay with the idea that I did, in fact, have choices. The main thing my intuition kept telling me was that I needed to create some breathing room in my life. A simple vacation or a week or two off wasn't going to be enough.

As I moved through the various stages of this major life change, things were still scary. I'd wake up in the middle of the night worrying that I'd never be given any professional opportunities again and that I'd be seen as a failure.

However, about nine months into the process, I began to see a pattern. My intuition would indicate a choice or change I needed to make. When I finally acceded and took the steps indicated, another idea or clue would be added. It was maddening not to be able to see where it was all headed. A new goal or intention didn't magically pop up during those initial stages, but I became comfortable with the idea that I was being led to something new and fullfilling. Ultimately, I had to learn to trust the process. It's actually been an incredible blessing to understand this. I know this awareness will be with me for the rest of my life.

Over the course of a two-year period, Jerry's life morphed into a mix of things he is really happy with. He's working part-time as an assistant professor for a local MBA program. He's still consulting for his former company as well as for an IT startup in his area. He's also taken the opportunity to take some painting classes and has a gallery showing soon. Jerry notes, "I just wish I hadn't worried so much. I had to learn that I was being guided each step along the way. I learned to trust that inner wisdom."

If you start work at age 20, work 40 hours a week and retire at age 65, you will have worked almost 100,000 hours. Wouldn't it be wonderful to spend those hours doing something you're passionate about—something that allows you to contribute your unique skill and interest to the world? If you don't begin now, when will you do it? John D. Rockefeller III put it this way on the Forbes.com Website: "The road to happiness lies in two simple principles: find what it is that interests you and that you can do well, and when you find it, put your whole soul into it—every bit of energy and ambition and natural ability that you have."

As Jerry indicated, it's not something that will likely happen overnight. All that is required of you right now is that you make a commitment to begin the process of uncovering what kind of work makes you happy. You don't have to know what it is or even how you'll make a living at it. Take it one step at a time. This is a process that will unfold in stages.

Are You Ready for a Change?

Answer each statement with yes or no.

_____1. I want to be in a different job next year.

_____2. I like my career, but feel I'm in the wrong position.

_____3. I long for the weekends when I can work on my hobbies or other interests.

_____4. There are other career choices that have always fascinated me and I'd like to check them out.

_____5. I need to find something new that's fresh and creative.

_____6. My work has become predictable and boring.

_____7. I find myself daydreaming a lot about switching careers.

_____8. I feel excited about a new career direction but can't figure out a way to earn a living at it.

_____9. I long for a way to make a contribution to my community but don't feel I can do it in my present work.

_____10. My life feels out of balance (too much work and not enough time for family, social, and personal interests).

_____11. I'm ready to work for myself. (Or, if you're already an entrepreneur: I'm ready to work for someone else.)

If you answered yes to most of the questions, you're definitely in a rut. Your intuition is telling you unambiguously that it's time for a career change. If you're not clear about your goals, your objective should be to *become* clear.

My clients often get stuck in that limbo space between "I know it's time to leave (or change) my work" and "I don't know what I want to do next." As it was for Jerry, it's an unsettling time for most people. We hate not knowing. The famous philosopher "Anonymous" once said, "The bend in the road is not the end of the road unless you refuse to make the turn." Here are some steps to get you started so you can make the right turn.

Acknowledge it's time for a change. You don't need to give up a job or career right now as the result of this insight. It's simply an inner step in the process of change. Consider letting friends and appropriate colleagues know what you're thinking and feeling. They may see that you possess strengths, skills, and interests that you haven't acknowledged in yourself.

Give yourself a period of exploration time. Depending on your situation, this can be a few weeks to a few years. You're using this time to consult your inner compass—your intuition. Of the possibilities in front of you, what feels exciting? Be willing to explore interests that may not make immediate sense in terms of a career choice. Within your dreams, interests, and aspirations, you'll find opportunity. It's as if your intuition gives you clues about the best path to follow even though your limited logical mind may not know where you're headed!

Commit to taking action steps. Motivational speaker and author Tony Robbins once observed, according to a quote on BrainyQuote.com, "You see, in life, lots of people know what to do, but few people actually do what they know. Knowing is not enough! You must take action." What are three things you could do this month that would give you information about your interest? Perhaps you could take a class, read a book, make an appointment with a career coach, or talk to someone who has a similar goal. It doesn't have to be a huge risk. When you commit to action, your intuition can begin to guide you. It puts options, possibility, and hope in your path.

Pay attention to synchronicity. We often fabricate limitations on our dreams for the future, saying things like, "I'd like to do _____, but I'm too old/young/uneducated/ inexperienced/etc." Your intuition isn't concerned with these limitations. When you're clear on what you want, it will begin to put the right circumstances and people in your path. Remember my story from Chapter 2? My business was launched by following an inner voice that directed me to sit next to a stranger at a funeral. An article she wrote about me for the *Boston Globe* newspaper skyrocketed my business to success. Weirder things have happened. They could happen to you, too. Be aware of what keeps showing up in your life. Those clues are pointing you in a new direction.

Ask your intuition open-ended questions. These might include:

> What would I enjoy doing for work?
>
> What next steps can I take that will lead me in the right direction?
>
> Who can I talk with that will help me with these choices?
>
> What could I do that would help others and be fun for me?

As you go about your day, pay attention to any inner nudges or impulses from your intuition that points you in a new direction.

Pay attention to those nudges. The intuitive voice that directs you to the next big thing in your life will likely not speak in a loud, booming voice announcing, "THIS IS IT!" Instead, you'll be guided by small "nudges" that make you think: "Hmmm…. This sounds interesting." "I notice that this company keeps showing up in my reading and conversations." "I'm having a recurring thought about X.

Perhaps I should research that a little further." "I keep thinking about [name of friend/colleague]. I should call and find out what she's up to these days."

Still feeling confused? Turn the page. In the next chapter I'll give you some tools you can use to team up with your intuition and discover a new direction.

Put Your Intuition to Work Tip

Your intuition is your inner compass. It delivers the message that you need to head in a new direction and shows you the best path to get there. Choose to follow it and it will lead you one step at a time to a better and more successful place.

| | | Put Your Intuition to Work Technique | | |
When Is It Time for Something New?

A definition of insanity: doing the same thing over and over again and expecting different results.

—Rita Mae Brown, writer

Life is full of transitions. The job that was once so compelling now feels draining. The new initiative you were thrilled to champion has become old school. Doors of opportunity used to fling open and now you can't seem to find the key. These are all important messages from your inner guidance that change is needed.

It can be a scary time because often we have to let go of what's not working before making room for anything new. Most of us are more comfortable when we have clear goals and an action plan for success. If you're finding that creative, innovative ideas and new direction are not coming to mind, you may have to clear out some space to allow room for a fresh approach.

If you've read this far in the book, you know that intuition is a clear guide to show you the most direct path to success. It can also tell you when it's time to change direction. When you're feeling positive and excited, that's your intuition giving you a "thumb's up." Following is a list of intuitive indicators that tell you you're headed in the wrong direction or that a change is needed.

I'm overwhelmed.

I feel depressed.

I've worked at something for a long time and nothing seems to go right.

People are not responding positively to my efforts.

I'm having trouble sleeping.

I'm constantly worried.

I'm trying too hard.

I frequently procrastinate.

I don't have a clear sense of direction.

I've lost confidence in myself and my abilities.

I feel like I constantly have to push to make things happen.

I've lost my motivation.

This endeavor is no longer fun and stimulating.

I'm frequently anxious.

I'm taking a lot of action steps to no avail.

I have recurrent accidents or illnesses.

Nothing I try seems to work.

I feel like I have to do it all myself.

I'm frequently tired.

Nothing seems interesting.

Clearly some of the above may indicate depression or some other illness. If you're experiencing many of these feelings and thoughts, you may want to get a professional opinion to rule out a medical condition. For the rest of you, if you mentally checked off five or more statements in the list, your intuition is trying to point you in a new direction. Not sure what to do next?

Chapter 15 | Dealing With Setbacks

When I'm old and dying, I plan to look back on my life and say "Wow, that was an adventure," not "Wow, I sure felt safe."

— Tom Preston-Werner, Github co-founder

"I now know I shouldn't make big life decisions when I'm stressed, overwhelmed and not sleeping well." That's how the conversation with my client Carol began. She described signing a contract to sell her small bed and breakfast inn after her husband passed away. "I allowed my fear to rule my decision and not my intuition."

Carol went on to tell me that her husband had died two years earlier after a long illness. The stress of trying to keep the B&B going by herself, managing the funeral, paying off medical bills, and dealing with insurance companies were enough to put her over the edge. She says:

Friends and colleagues kept offering to help me, but I just couldn't accept their assistance. I thought I could tough it out. I was smart and capable and somehow convinced myself I should be able to handle it all.

A fellow inn owner made an offer to buy my property several months after my husband died. It was a reasonable price. I thought, at first, that this was the answer to my prayers. I could get out of the business, sell the house, and be free. I just wasn't paying attention to that proverbial gut feeling that was sending up warning flares all over the place. I kept having the feeling that I couldn't trust this guy. Something didn't feel right, but I couldn't put my finger on it so I ignored it. My logical brain said that my lawyer had drawn up a good contract that appeared to protect me. I consistently chalked up those intuitive forebodings to simple stress and nerves.

Looking back there were so many cautionary signs that I simply explained away. His deposit check didn't clear at first. However, he had a reasonable sounding explanation for that. While the negotiations were going on, I made a few calls for references. The people I reached all said the right things, but they were said without a lot of enthusiasm. I should have made note of that! My buyer also shared various anecdotes about his experiences and in hindsight, I noted that he was always the victim in his stories. It was always everyone else's fault. Any one of these issues should have made me pay attention! Unfortunately, I didn't.

The short version of the story is that the new owner never intended to honor the contract. He continued to use my name and the name of my business in his advertising instead of "Under New Management" and a different business name that we'd agreed to. I began seeing reviews about the place being unclean and where people weren't treated well. It just went downhill from there. I've spent a fortune on lawyers fees in addition to the time in court. It's been an expensive lesson in the importance of trusting my intuition.

Find Your Alternative Course of Action

Carol has managed to make lemons out of lemonade in this situation. She read me a quote by Mary Kay Ash, the founder of Mary Kay Cosmetics, that said, "For every failure, there's an alternative course of action. You just have to find it. When you come to a roadblock, take a detour." She decided to follow that advice and not keep dwelling on her setbacks.

While the legal issues were still unfolding, she began to work as a coach/consultant to others who wanted to buy or sell their inns and B&B's. She says, "I love working with people who are in the midst of change and transition. The hospitality industry is one that I'm familiar with, and I've found a new passion in working in a different end of this business. You can be sure that one of my main messages to all my clients is to trust your gut!"

What Does Accurate Intuition Look and Feel Like?

If you're facing a potential big change or decision like Carol did, what should accurate intuitive guidance look and feel like? In other words, how do you know when you're simply engaging in wishful idealistic thinking instead of receiving a true intuitive message? Here are some factors to consider:

A Small Amount of Anxiety Is Normal

If we're honest, we all experience a degree of fear when we decide to do something new. A change will likely require that you develop new skills and become more proficient with ones you already have. You're moving outside of your comfort zone into unknown territory.

Is your apprehension more pronounced than it normally would be given the change you're anticipating? You're the only one who can answer that. Think back to other times of transition in your life. How did you feel as you were going through them? Was your intuition giving you the "go ahead" then? Did you trust it? How did it work out?

Just Focus on What's Next

Most decisions don't require a flying leap of faith. How could you take some small steps toward your decision? For example, you may be contemplating a career change. Do some information-gathering. This might be a class you take, a colleague you speak to, or a book you read. If you're still feeling motivated and excited about the change, that's your intuition giving you a green light. Take a bigger step.

If, like Carol, you're hitting roadblocks or continuing to have uneasy feelings, pay attention! Depending on the situation, you may simply need to take a detour or just stop where you are and not move forward for the time being.

It May Not Be the Right Time

Intuition doesn't always give a clear yes or no. Sometimes it gives a qualified maybe. The implications of this message are that progress appears stalled. I have a tendency to be rather impatient. However, over the years I've learned that when I can be patient and wait, things have a way of working out. When I push the envelope and try to force things to happen, I find I've stepped out of the flow and the ease that usually characterize intuitively inspired decisions and action.

Be Clear About the Outcome You Want

In Carol's story, her initial goal was to sell the business to an appropriate buyer and to do it in such a way that she'd have enough money to transition easily into a new career. Admittedly, because she was fatigued and overwhelmed, she allowed the goal to become simply "sell the business."

Writer Aldous Huxley was quoted on azquotes.com as saying, "When life appears to be working against you, when your luck is down, when the supposedly wrong people show up, or when you slip up and return to old, self-defeating habits, recognize the signs that you're out of harmony with intention."

If you're feeling fearful or anxious about a course of action, step back and ask yourself if you're clear about what you want. Like Carol was, you may be headed in a direction you don't really want to go. If that's the case, take a break, slow down, and rethink what you truly want.

What to Do if You're Off Track

If You Get Off Track, Be Willing to Change

As Yogi Berra said, "If you come to a fork in the road, take it!" What are you doing that's on the mark? If one way doesn't work for you, be ready to go another. Many times, the road to success is found by taking a detour. Sometimes we get overly focused on getting to our goals through a well-trodden or familiar path.

It's worth noting that many of the people I interviewed for this book mentioned detours and other crises that ultimately served to get them on track. With enough distance, almost all of them were grateful for the setbacks because it allowed a whole new and more interesting life to emerge. They invariably mentioned that following their intuition was the guide that led them back to success.

Look Ahead, Rather Than Back

Sometimes a shift in perspective is all it takes to get you out of a state of anxiety. Napoleon Hill wrote in his book *Think and Grow Rich*, "Every adversity, every failure, every heartache carries with it the seed of an equal or greater benefit." Sometimes we spend more time looking at the failure. Your focus needs to be on where you're heading next.

I was speaking with a client recently who was contemplating going back to school for a master's degree at 53 years old. She was the director of a high-profile non-profit organization and had been in this position for 15 years. She knew it was time to leave and yet was consumed with anxiety about whether the program she'd been accepted into was the right choice. Was her intuition telling her not to go? I suggested she think of her life a year from now and ask, "How will you feel if you're still in your current job and you didn't go back to school?" Her instant reply? "Disappointed." Her response served to soften her anxiety. It made her realize that she was, in fact, heading in the right direction.

Give Yourself a Performance Review

When you've put a lot of hard work into an endeavor and it's not going as you planned, it's not easy to step back and assess the situation. Is there something that you feel you're "failing" at in your life? The following questions will help you put some perspective on your experience:

What can you learn from this?

What are you doing right?

What outcome will make you feel you're successful?

Where did this begin to go wrong?

What do you wish you had done differently?

What is your intuition telling you to do about this situation?

What are you not listening to?

Are there warning signs you're ignoring?

What do you know you should do?

After answering these questions, do you feel there's a different way to approach your project or endeavor? Depending on the issue, you have several options. You could:

ʔ   Quit.

ʔ   Persevere.

ʔ   Alter your course.

ʔ   Put the project on hold for a period of time.

ʔ   Try something new.

ʔ   Ask for advice from someone who has been successful in a similar endeavor.

ʔ   Work on your project part-time.

ʔ   Discuss the situation with others who may be involved.

Which of these options feels best to you? You can choose more than one, and your intuition may present you with even more choices than listed.

It's Okay to Fail

Thomas J. Watson was the founder of IBM. He was one of the richest men of his time and considered one of the world's greatest salesmen when he died in 1956. I thought his words, on ThinkExist.com, might provide some comfort for those experiencing a setback: "Would you like me to give you a formula for success? It's quite simple, really. Double your rate of failure. You are thinking of failure as the enemy of success. But it isn't at all. You can be discouraged by failure or you can learn from it. So go ahead and make mistakes. Make all you can. Because remember, that's where you will find success."

I've often observed that the clients who quickly get back on their feet after a setback have an unusual mindset. They say to themselves something along the lines of "I've discovered something that didn't work well for me. I've learned from it. Let me take this experience, figure out my next steps and move forward." The clients that stay mired in the setback tend to label themselves a failure rather than their experience. Which one would you choose?

And here's a slightly more modern version of the same advice from Richard Branson from his Virgin.com site: "My mother always taught me never to look back in regret but to move on to the next thing. The amount of time people waste dwelling on failures rather than putting that energy into another project, always amazes me. I have fun running all the Virgin businesses—so a setback is never a bad experience, just a learning curve."

I love that way of viewing a setback. Not a failure or, even a bad experience. It's a "learning curve." It sounds like Richard Branson is a true gut truster. And, of course, mothers are always right!

Put Your Intuition to Work Tip
Intuition doesn't always give a clear yes or no. Sometimes it gives a qualified maybe. When you try to force things to happen, you may find that you step out of the flow and the ease that usually characterize intuitively inspired decisions and action.

{ }

Chapter 16 | Success Secrets of Intuitive People

In moments of doubt and fear, I now trust the guide that's inside of me. This inner guide is more powerful than any external influence and has the ability to dissipate my fears. Many of my failures came from not trusting myself.

—Faisal Hoque, founder of Shadoka

Many of us take the path of least resistance in life. We're out of work, a job is offered, and we might as well take it. Or an opportunity has opened up in another department. It offers a change of pace and more money, and it's clearly a promotion. You decide you'll take it. Why not? The cliché that "If you don't know where you're going, you'll probably end up there" holds true in so many situations. We fail to check in with our intuition and ask, "Is this a good decision?" How will you know if you don't ask? And if you do ask, how will you know the answer? (Aren't you glad you asked?!)

Marilyn is one of my clients. At our first meeting she explained:

I took the first job offer I received after graduating from college. Since then, I've been promoted many times, changed jobs twice and continue to make more money and achieve significant career advancement. Everyone who knows me would say I'm successful. I'm 38 years old, married, mortgage, two kids to support and it finally occurred to me that I've really never asked myself what makes my heart sing. I've just grabbed the next obvious opportunity as it came my way. No wonder I'm unhappy!

Moving Toward Happiness

You can sit in on our initial meeting where we discussed many of the themes in this chapter.

What's Wrong With Your Current Situation?

Often the answer to the question "what's next?" is a little too overwhelming and not easily answered. Sometimes it helps to understand what you don't want before figuring out what you do want.

Marilyn had a ready list of items that weren't working for her in her present occupation:

I don't like being in a huge corporation. I feel like a cog in a wheel. The long hours are really tough on me because I'm not spending enough time with family, friends or even myself. I have a new boss who is a micromanager, and I'm someone who really thrives on autonomy. Also, I'm an extrovert and my current job requires spending hours at my desk doing detailed analysis.

Marilyn's comments may sound like one long whine, but asking yourself what you don't want or don't like about your current situation will provide valuable information about what you *do* want.

Get Clear About What You Want

Look at the list of statements about what's not working in your current job or work. Try turning them around. Following are a few examples based on the conversation with Marilyn:

"I no longer want to work long hours" becomes "I want a job where I can be home in time to see my son's afternoon baseball games" or "I'd love to be at a company that allows me to telecommute several days a week."

"I'm an extrovert who dislikes doing detailed analysis" becomes "I'd love to do work where I'm out meeting customers at least part of the week. I could also imagine coaching, speaking, or training as part of my job. Anything that gets me out with people."

Being clear about what you want is often the first step in being able to create it. Set aside for now the question of *how* you will get this work or job. That will come later. Don't put the cart before the horse. It's difficult to focus on *how* you're going to get someplace before figuring out *where* it is you're heading!

What Would Be Fun, Interesting, or Exciting?

Begin to play around with the idea of creating something new. I jokingly tell people that if I can make a living at what *I* do, it's possible to make a living doing anything! When you discover the answer to *what* (you love to do) your intuition will provide the insight that will give you the clues to discover the *how* (to make a living at it).

Gerry Harrington, president of New Spirituality Communications, adds these words of wisdom: "Go for things that are aligned with your values, even if there's nothing like it anywhere in the world. Your heart doesn't invest in a compromise." (You can find this quote and others on the value of persistence at Entrepreneur.com.)

Say No to "Buts"

You've probably had many creative and inspirational ideas about things that you'd like to do, achieve, or accomplish. Perhaps you, like Marilyn, have had a fantasy of trying some entirely new type of work. Maybe you've daydreamed about a trip you wanted to take. Or you may have relegated a passion for something into "just a hobby" instead of allowing for the possibility you could make a living at it.

If you haven't taken action on those ideas, I'd be willing to bet you've fallen under the tyranny of a powerful word: *but*. That word puts the kibosh on anything that preceded it. "I could do this, this, and this!" you think excitedly. That's your intuition serving up some creative and innovative ideas that will point you in a new and successful direction.

Unfortunately, your logical mind joins in at just that moment with "But how can you do that? You can't! Your idea is nonsense. It's too hard (expensive, requires more education or training, blah blah blah). Here's an example of a "yes but" that Marilyn came up with: "I'd love to be more involved with customer service training. The idea of making us more customer friendly really appeals to me. But... I'd have to go back to school to get a degree."

Shift Your Thinking

There's nothing wrong with the fact that your logical mind jumps in and wants to have some input into how you'll achieve these hopes and dreams. After all, it has a role to play in helping you succeed! However, you don't want it to dampen your enthusiasm and inspirational sparks by leaping in too soon. Try saying things like "Let me be open to possibilities," "What steps could I take to make this happen?" "Where can I begin?" or "If this idea were possible, what would I do next?"

Make the First Step a Small Step

The trick to breaking the habit of defeatist thinking is twofold:

1. Just begin.
2. Start small.

Take a first step toward what you feel excited about, and then take another one and another one. Remain centered in the present. You don't have to know exactly *how* your dreams will manifest. Trust your inner direction from your intuition. When you follow your passion, excitement, and inner knowing, you'll discover what makes you happy and fulfilled. When you know what you want, there's a clear path to achieve it. Your guidance will show you the way.

Keep an Intuitive Career Ideas Journal

Jotting down ideas as they come to you is one of the most helpful ways to open your mind to allow intuitive idea generation. Following are some questions to get you started. Clients have approached this list in varied ways. Marilyn bought a purse-size notebook and every day she focused on answering just one question, writing down the ideas as they came to her. Others have taken a several-days-long retreat where they could take time with their answers. Whatever works for you is fine.

What are your gifts?

- What life achievements or accomplishments have made you feel proud?
- What abilities do you have that people praise?
- What tasks or skills come easily to you? Make a list of things you do well.
- What were you good at as a child?
- If someone were to give your eulogy, what contributions would they say you have made to the world?

What are you passionate about?

- What are you doing when you lose track of time?
- If you had enough money to take a year off, what would you do with your free time?
- Is there something you want to devote your life to?
- How can you help others by doing what you enjoy?
- If you could make one contribution to the world before you die, what would it be?
- What do you want to teach others?
- What excites or angers you most about our world?

What are your values?

- ⊦ What matters most to you? Consider things like autonomy, humanity, creativity, kindness, power, wealth, spirituality, knowledge, leadership, community, beauty, and intellectual pursuits.

- ⊦ Think of someone you admire. What is it about their life that you appreciate? What values do you think they hold?

What's fun for you?

- ⊦ Make a list of 20, 50, or a hundred things you love to do.

- ⊦ How would you spend your ideal day/week/month/year?

- ⊦ If you were to win the lottery and money were no longer a factor, what would you do?

- ⊦ Do you enjoy doing things by yourself? With a partner? A team?

- ⊦ What kind of setting do you like to be in? Are you an outdoor person or more comfortable behind a desk? Consider your surroundings when imagining your fun, ideal life.

As you look at your answers, are there any themes that emerged? Were there any "a-ha" moments that caught you by surprise? Once you have your list of accomplishments, competencies, values, and passions, there are a few more steps. The answer to the question "How can I do something I enjoy and make a living at it?" may not come overnight.

One of the qualities I believe we must develop in order to use our intuition wisely is that of patience. Napoleon Hill, the author of the classic book *Think and Grow Rich,* makes a good case for this very attribute when he states, "Patience, persistence and perspiration make an unbeatable combination for success."

Need another idea? Try a brief check-in with your intuition at the end of the day. It's also a great opportunity to prepare for the next day.

G Is for Gratitude

What happened today that you're grateful for? Was there a business opportunity that came your way? A good conversation with your partner? Perhaps it was the simple notion that you're alive, healthy, and happy? When you take note of these things, you'll find they magically increase.

U Is for Unlimited

Tomorrow is full of unlimited possibilities and potential. As you prepare for sleep, this is an opportunity to put a request out to your intuitive advisor. What would you like to see happen during the next day? Write down three ideas of what an ideal day would look and feel like. You're basically asking for guidance. "What could I do to create this ideal day?"

T Is for Trust

Expect to get an answer from your intuition. You may have an idea pop into your mind immediately. You might find you have a dream that provides a clue, or the answer may come as you drink your morning beverage. Be on the lookout for those intuitive messages.

Sometimes intuitive answers come in "sneaky" ways. Your attention gets drawn to an article in the morning paper and the answer is there. An unnoticed billboard you drive by every morning suddenly alerts you to a possible solution to a problem. And we've all had the experience of turning on the radio or podcast at just the right moment to hear the words of wisdom we seek. When it's the right answer, you'll likely feel one of the following: settled, relieved, expansive, reassured, or simply calm.

What happened to Marilyn my client from the beginning of the chapter? She stayed with her current company and pitched them on a new position. She's now a customer service liaison. She follows up with current customers to make sure they've had a successful experience with her company. She communicates suggestions for improvements and relays praises back to headquarters. She reports she couldn't be happier!

Put Your Intuition to Work Tip
It's not always easy to answer the question "What do I want?" Begin to think about what you don't want first. What drains your batteries? Start there and clear out the energy blockages. Once you do that, you'll make room for more energy-producing ideas.

| | | Put Your Intuition to Work Technique | | |
7 Ways to Jump-Start Your Intuition
When You Have 5 Minutes or Less

Good instincts usually tell you what to do long before your head has figured it out.

—Michael Burke, professor of psychology and business,
Tulane University

Meditate. Simply calm your mind by focusing on your breathing. Repeat a word or phrase that makes you feel relaxed, such as *peace, "It's all good,"* or *calm.* Buddhists call this mindfulness. When we slow down for even a few moments, we cultivate our creativity, intuition, and inner peace.

Ask your intuition questions. Framing the questions to evoke more than a yes or no answer will elicit a more informative response. For example, "How can we get more people to sign up for our seminar next month?" or "What could we do to create more brand recognition of product X?" Spend your remaining time writing any and all answers that pop into your mind. Don't censor or judge the responses until you've completed the exercise.

Ask for an image. If you're trying to make a decision about something and your logical, rational mind is running amok, close your eyes and ask for a symbolic picture of the solution. Intuitive answers often come through a visual representation.

Get moving. Simply standing up and moving will bring more oxygen to your brain and help you think more clearly. Put your work on hold and go for a brisk walk. Chances are good that simply getting away from your desk and taking your focus off of your problem will generate a creative idea or two.

Daydream. Think about the challenge, decision, or problem you're facing. In your mind's eye, visualize yourself in a situation where you're dealing with this issue and expect an answer. Perhaps someone comes up to you and provides the solution in a conversation. Or you might see a book, banner, note, or some other communication that gives you a clue to the response you're seeking. While it may seem odd or silly, you'd be surprised how many wonderful solutions come forth this way.

Notice how it feels. You're trying to make a decision about whether to invest in an expensive new piece of equipment your factory manager is asking for. He's presented a good case with all the facts and figures. You're still not sure. Close your eyes and imagine saying yes. How does that decision feel? How do you feel emotionally? Heavy, weighty, depressing feelings generally indicate "Don't go with this." Up, energizing, enthusiastic, positive emotions point to an affirmative response.

What's your body say? The ancient Chinese believed that wisdom resides in the stomach. An early example of "trust your gut," perhaps? If your stomach becomes nervous at the thought of a particular direction, pay attention. Other physical sensations may provide clues as well. Perhaps you break into a sweat when faced with a choice you know isn't right. Others might feel a tingly zing up their spine. On the other hand, a warm, cozy feeling might indicate you're heading in the right direction. Only you know your body and can read its signs. When you're comfortable translating its messages, you'll have tapped into your inner genius.

{ }

Chapter 17 | What's a Dream Worth?

I've realized that most of my best ideas have followed a good night's sleep.

—Thomas Edison, American inventor and businessman

Jean describes herself as a high school dropout who's now the president and CEO of her $25 million a year service business. She credits a dream she had when she was 28 years old as part of what got her started on her path to success. She says, "I was in a grocery store and noticed that there were coins scattered all down the aisles. It struck me as incredibly odd that everyone was walking right past these gold pieces while I was busy picking them up as fast as I could."

She awoke from the dream with a powerful thought: "I see opportunities where others do not." She describes this dream as helping her understand that she had a Divine calling. She felt that she was "wired for business." The dream provided both the catalyst and courage to start her company.

Famous Dreamers

Jean isn't alone in finding dreams helpful. Successful people in all walks of life have pointed to their dreams as a rich source of ideas, solutions, and creative direction. Pro golfer Jack Nicklaus credits a dream with helping him improve his golf swing after an extended and embarrassing professional slump. The day after his dream, he improved his game by 10 strokes.

In the book *Dreamland: Adventures in the Strange Science of Sleep,* author David K. Randall writes about the morning that former Beatle Paul McCartney woke up from a dream with the tune to the song "Yesterday" running through his mind: "It was just all there," he said. "A complete thing, I couldn't believe it." It rapidly became a pop standard (2,500 versions), covered by everyone from Frank Sinatra to Marianne Faithfull. Fifty-plus years later it's still the most played song on the radio.

On average, you can dream anywhere from one to two hours every night. Moreover, you can have four to seven dreams in one night. There are many well-documented tales of creative solutions springing from dreams. In an average lifetime, you would have spent a total of about six years of it dreaming. That is more than 2,100 days. You might as well take advantage of the fabulous information in your dreams!

German physiologist Otto Leowi credits a dream with enabling him to prove that nerve impulses were chemical rather than electrical. He won the Nobel Prize for this discovery. Rolling Stones guitarist Keith Richards said the riff in "(I Can't Get No) Satisfaction" came to him in his sleep. And the 19th-century chemist Dmitri Mendeleev reportedly dreamed up the periodic table of elements.

Elias Howe was trying to invent a practical sewing machine. He was experiencing difficulty with the needle design until a solution came to him in a dream. A tribe of savages captured him and brought him before their king. The monarch roared, "Elias Howe, I command you on pain of death to finish this machine at once." In his dream, the warriors were thrusting their spears toward him in a menacing manner. Suddenly he noticed that at the end of these spears were eye-shaped holes. He awoke from his dream, sprang out of bed, and whittled a needle with an eye in the point. It was a small but incredibly significant change that revolutionized an industry.

Raymond Kurzweil is a pioneer in the fields of optical character recognition (OCR), text-to-speech synthesis, speech recognition technology, and electronic musical keyboards. He's also the author of several books on health and technology. What makes him so productive? He's quoted in an interview on the American Foundation for the Blind Website saying:

I do my most creative work, literally, sort of in bed, a lucid dreaming process.... [W]hile I'm dreaming, that's the most creative time. All the sensors in your head are relaxed. I think about the issue again in the morning and can write a whole chapter of a new book, write a speech or come up with a new invention in just a few minutes.

A dream is also credited with saving the Dupont Corporation millions of dollars. Their Kevlar vests were in huge demand during the Gulf War and a special high-speed machine was set up to create them. Unfortunately for both DuPont and the soldiers, it kept breaking down. The engineers couldn't figure out what was going wrong until one of them had a dream. He dreamed that he had become part of the machine and saw water spraying around indiscriminately and hoses collapsing. When he awoke, he immediately set to work creating some springs that would help keep the hoses open. His dream solution saved the day and probably saved many lives as well.

Suppose you could go to sleep at night and come up with solutions to your work-related problems. It's really a very cushy job! The requirements? Just a nice soft bed, a little thinking and writing, a pen and paper on the nightstand. After that, you just close your eyes and dream. Upon awakening in the morning, be willing to write down your insights. That's it! Need more detail? Here are some things to do to help you use your sleeping state to help you resolve problems and come up with creative solutions.

Sleep on It

Sometimes a challenge feels a bit overwhelming and it's difficult to get your logical, rational mind out of the way to listen for the intuitive insights. You may find you get the best answers when you turn your brain off and go to sleep.

Keep a Dream Journal

This doesn't need to be anything fancy. A notebook or pad of paper beside your bed works great. If you're not concerned with waking your bedmate, using the recorder on your phone could work as well. Before you go to sleep, write a few paragraphs about the decision you're trying to make or the issue you're seeking insight about. You're basically trying to get a data dump from the left side of your brain onto the page.

Summarize the Issue

Read the paragraphs you've written and condense it into a one-sentence question. Example: "Should I pursue this new career direction?" or "How can we speed up the manufacturing process of our widgets?" Others have found it easier to simply ask for information about a concern. Example: "I need information about increasing sales." or "I would like a dream about a prosperous new direction for my business."

Ask the Question or State the Concern as You Drift to Sleep

Tell yourself that you'll remember a dream that will provide the answer(s) to this question. As you doze off, repeat your phrase softly to yourself, with the mental expectation of receiving an answer. If your mind wanders, gently bring it back to the question.

Wake Up Slowly

Five minutes after the end of the dream, half the content is forgotten. After 10 minutes, 90 percent is lost. As you wake up try not to come *fully* awake at first. Ask yourself, "Did I have a dream about my concern?" Don't get out of bed. In fact, move as little as possible when you're in the middle of dream recall.

Record the Dreams or Dream Fragments

Even if you don't remember the entire dream, jot down the fragments. Answers in dreams don't always announce themselves in an obvious way. They'll show up through symbolic images, metaphor, feelings, and sensations.

Interpret the Dream

There are vast libraries of books on the subject of dream interpretation. However, many tend to reduce everything to a universal symbol. A fire might signify a romantic evening to one person but to you it might be a sign of danger. *You're* the expert on you and your dreams. Here are some items to consider to help you jumpstart your interpretation:

Look for the solution. Is there an immediate answer you've received upon awakening? What can you take away from the dream and use in your current situation? Is there any part of your dream that leaps out at you as important and worthy of some further reflection?

Identify the symbols. Are there dream symbols or metaphors that pertain to your question from the night before? How might these be relevant to your question and answer? What pops into your mind when you think about these symbols? Who or what in your life do they remind you of?

Describe the dream out loud. A dream's meaning can become clear when you verbalize it, because we often use plays on words to form pictures. For example, I once had a dream about a pain in my foot. I kept saying, "It hurts to put my foot down." I realized I was unconsciously referring to my inability to set appropriate boundaries and limits on a colleague at work. In other words, I wasn't "putting my foot down" in this situation. You might also describe your dream in the first person, present tense. This will often evoke some overlooked piece of information.

Still having trouble remembering your dreams? A few more tips follow.

Create a Dream Map

The most common complaint about remembering your dreams is that you only remember a dream fragment. If that's you, consider creating a "dream map," similar to mind mapping. For example, if you dream about a falling building, but the only thing you really remember is the building, write the word *building* in a mind-map bubble. Then draw a branch off of it and see what word associations and information comes to you.

I did this for a falling building dream that I had. (It's a common dream!) One of the bubbles had the word *fear* and one the phrase *out of control*. Another one said *offices*. More details came as I wrote each word. The way I interpreted it was that I was experiencing a lot of anxiety about a change I was making in my business direction. Recognizing that was helpful in deciding to take things a little slower and do some more research before proceeding further.

The more you remember about each part of the dream, the more bubbles you can add. Sometimes parts of the dream may come to you at a later point in the day. If it feels like an important dream, keep notes on any further information that comes forth. Once you get it all mapped out, you may be surprised at how much you actually remember. You don't have to worry about the sequence of events, just the words and feelings. By doing this, you may be able to fill in the gaps of your fuzzy dream.

Shift Your Position Slowly as You Wake

Dr. Patricia Garfield is a well-known dream researcher. She suggests that prepping your mind to remember your dreams is essential for dream recollection, but you must remember to prep your body as well. For instance, if you typically sleep in the same position and can't seem to remember your dreams, slowly roll over on to your opposite sleeping side and lie there for a moment, asking, "What did I dream about?" She's one of many dream researchers that advocate waking naturally without a cacophonous alarm clock.

If all else fails, keep trying. You may receive help in your dream in more ways than you know. In a fascinating article on the Website ASDreams.org, author John Steinbeck is quoted as saying, "It is a common experience that a problem difficult at night is resolved in the morning after the committee of sleep has worked on it."

May you and your committee have a good night's sleep!

Put Your Intuition to Work Tip

If you're trying to make a decision, ask for a dream. Ask the question or state the concern as you drift off to sleep. Tell yourself that you'll remember a dream that will provide the answer(s) to this question. Keep a pad of paper and a pen beside your bed and jot down anything you remember from the dream when you awaken.

Chapter 18 | How to Blink

*I believe that the task of making sense of ourselves and our behavior
requires that we acknowledge there can be as much value in the blink of an
eye as in months of rational analysis.*

—Malcolm Gladwell, author and speaker

Malcolm Gladwell's bestselling book *Blink: The Power of
Thinking Without Thinking* has popularized a form of intuition that Gladwell calls "thin-slicing." He speculates that we
are able to make highly accurate decisions with very limited
amounts of information. "Thin-slicing refers to the ability of
our subconscious to find patterns in situations and people
based on very narrow slices of experience," he explains.

Deciding to accept a new job is one of the more significant
decisions you may have to make. Most of us do our research
by talking to colleagues about the position, making inquiries,
going on interviews, reading background about the company,
and so forth. It's the way you're supposed to do it, right?

However, if you're really honest with yourself, you probably had a gut feeling about the position right from the start. It
might have been when you walked into the room for an interview, or the way you felt when you drove your car into the company parking lot. Perhaps it came even sooner, when you first
heard about the job. Instead of trusting that instant when you
knew in your gut the position was right for you (or not), you
probably proceeded to do your homework and gather information. After all, is it really possible to accurately know something in the blink of an eye?

Gladwell posits that we understand a great deal without necessarily being able to explain why and how. We can

frequently make some of our best decisions in mere seconds. We think without thinking. While he doesn't use the word *intuition* in his book, he describes a form of it that is based on sizing up situations and determining how we feel about a person or situation based not on new information, but rather on our accumulated experiences.

How to Thin-Slice

What's My First Impression?

Train yourself to ask this question before beginning the process of analysis and research. Note your response and store it away for future reference. The answer you receive shouldn't preclude doing your homework on the subject at hand. However, when you use your intuition first and hone your skill through repetition, you'll find you have quick, ready, and accurate insight at your disposal whenever you need it.

What Do I Need to Know?

Asking this question alerts you to additional information. It gives you insight into what may be just outside your level of conscious awareness. What's wrong (or right) with the situation you're observing? It's helpful to stay emotionally neutral or open when you ask this question. What insight comes to you naturally? Simply observe it. Don't judge it.

What's the Best Course of Action?

What pops into your mind when you ask this question? There's a big difference between using your intuition and impulsive, irresponsible decision-making. Again, it takes practice. If you were just beginning to learn to play a piano, you wouldn't expect yourself to be a concert pianist within the first week. So it is with intuition. You learn by a series of small steps. How do you experience an intuitive yes response? How does an intuitively conveyed "Don't go in that direction" feel to you? The answers present themselves in quick flashes, a sudden insight, an unexpected feeling, or a certain knowing. Only *you* have the key to unlock how it communicates in your own body, mind, and spirit. Once you find that key, you'll find success.

Thinking Fast and Quick

How do scientists view this whole concept of intuition and "thin-slicing" in particular? Does it come from our mind? Our experience? In reality, they've yet to find anything in the body that defines either intuition or, more generally, consciousness. Where does "the mind" as we know it exist?

Dr. Larry Dossey is an author and internist who lectures widely on the topics of spirituality and science. He suggests there is an aspect of our mind that defies space and time limitations. He uses the term *non-local* mind, a concept coined and used in contemporary quantum physics.

He writes in his book *Recovering the Soul*:

The non-local model is not confined in space and time to the brain and body, although it may work through the brain and body. And it is not confined to the present moment. Infinite, and by inference immortal, eternal, omnipresent—all of these are consequences of anything that is non-local, not just mind. As a result, if mind is non-local, there is one mind, or Universal Mind, which the West has regarded as the Soul.

This opens up interesting questions about intuition. My position in this book is that intuition comes from two general sources. The first is a quick processing of subconscious information. You might use this when you're making a hiring decision and you observe the applicant's style of clothes, manner of speaking, and body language, and come up with an instinctual impression of them. The second type of intuition is what

Dossey is alluding to. We have access to a larger, more infinite pool of knowledge through the non-local mind and we connect to it through our intuitive knowing.

Bell's Theorem is named for its author, Irish physicist John Stewart Bell. He demonstrated mathematically that the speed at which information can travel from point A to point B is not, as Albert Einstein's Special Theory of Relativity stated, limited to the speed of light or less. Bell's Theorem says that this connection is not just a theory, but actually exists in the real world. Dr Nick Herbert, also a physicist and author of the book *Quantum Reality*, maintains that when A connects to B, non-locally, nothing crosses the intervening space, and that no matter how far A is from B, the connection is instantaneous.

How does all this relate to intuition? You have a connection to an amazing wealth of information at your disposal through your extended consciousness. When you're thinking about how your factory is doing in Singapore or wondering how to make a sales pitch to your client in Boston, you can pick up information instantly. You don't need to be there in person observing what's going on. It also explains my work as an intuitive and my seemingly implausible ability to tell you, with no rational way of knowing, what will motivate a decision-maker to choose your company over the competition.

Interestingly, this information about the non-local mind is not new. It's reminiscent of what philosopher Patanjali wrote in the second century BC (and found more recently on ThinkExist.com):

When you are inspired by some great purpose, some extraordinary project, all your thoughts break their bonds. Your mind transcends limitations, your consciousness expands in every direction, and you find yourself in a new, great and wonderful world. Dormant forces, faculties and talents become alive, and you discover yourself to be a greater person by far than you ever dreamed yourself to be.

Is It Your Mind, Your Gut, or. . ?

Lance is an engineer who specializes in large turbine-powered generators. He's often called upon to join a "S.W.A.T." team whose mission is to track down and eliminate equipment problems. The rational and logical approach usually rules with this group, yet Lance has become a convert to the more intuitive approach. He is, however, the first to admit he doesn't know where the information comes from. He relates this story:

Several years ago, on a "mission" in England, the team found itself in the middle of a fascinating puzzle where a collective gut instinct provided the only solution.

It seems that a recently rebuilt turbine was showing an unexplainable increase of temperature. The customer was happy with the power output, but because of the abnormally high temperature, the unit would have to be checked out to satisfy safety requirements.

Normally, we'd have shut the entire unit down so we could get inside for a thorough examination. But the "patient" weighed twenty tons and was running at a thousand degrees Fahrenheit, which meant it would take three days to cool down enough to allow us to begin work. Add another nine days of outage to do the investigation, it could have cost the customer millions of dollars.

I felt instinctively that there wasn't any significant issue with this turbine. But could the first stage turbine blades have been installed backward? Though we didn't really know what was actually going on inside that monster, we collectively just knew—really knew— that those blades were not installed incorrectly and that the unit was safe.

Since engineers don't readily confess to "feelings" about things, I wrote into my report that we were confident that (not "we felt" that) the blades were fine and the unit would continue to generate power without generating problems.

Three and a half years later the unit was still running like new. But we were enormously curious about what might have caused the temperature aberration, so, after high-fives all around, we began an animated half-way-around-the-world co-investigation. The unit was to be open for just a few hours, so we feverishly gathered data long into the night.

Bottom line: We found nothing. But most important, we found nothing wrong*! So in the end, our collective gut feeling was verified.*

Later, after looking closely at all the data we'd gathered, we concluded the errant indication was most likely caused by an unusual flow pattern around the temperature sensor. The result? The combined intuition of my team had saved an important customer tens of millions of dollars.

Don't Overthink It

Maybe you're not dealing with turbine-powered generators and a potential 10-to-20-million-dollar decision like our engineer, Lance. But you've got a big decision to make. Perhaps you're responsible to thousands of shareholders or to the members of your immediate family. The business decisions you make are equally critical and capable of changing lives for better—or for worse.

The decision you're about to make has been well thought through. You've done due diligence in gathering the facts, the data, others' opinions. You're ready to make that hugely important hire; to pitch that account you not only want, but need; to commit funds to develop that new product that will absolutely clobber the competition. And yet, you're not sure.

There's something nibbling away at the back of your brain—a little cinch worm of uncertainty—making you hesitate, giving you pause.

Now is the time to sit back, relax, close your eyes, and ask the following question: Is the decision I'm about to make a *good* decision? Ask it as if someone besides you is listening. You're asking your intuition an important question and your intuition is going to give you an answer. It may come in the form of words, symbols, images, feelings. Most people get a "feeling" that something is good or bad, right or wrong. The Japanese call it *haragei*, which translates to "belly sensitivity" or "stomach art." We call it "gut instinct."

Choices are a fact of life. What makes a life successful is the ability to make more good choices than bad choices. Your intuition is there to guide you, like a trusty compass, to the choices that are best for *you*. Take advantage of it, listen to what it tells you, then act accordingly and expect success.

Put Your Intuition to Work Tip
Get to know how your own inner guidance systems works. When you're going in the wrong direction, how does your intuition let you know? Conversely, what signals do you get that say "Yes! Good decision!"? Pay attention to your own unique intuitive signals, especially when you're making relatively low-risk decisions. These same signals will be there when you have to make a fast, quick, and significant decision in your life.

| | | Put Your Intuition to Work Technique | | |
Not Your Typical Coin Toss

No great discovery was ever made without a bold guess.
—Sir Isaac Newton, English physicist and mathematician

This is a great technique to use when the stakes aren't too high. I wouldn't necessarily use this method for major decisions like whether to sell the company, quit your job, or move across the continent. But then, that's just me!

Think about a decision you're trying to make. Form it in your mind as a yes or no question. Examples are:

Should I take the position with XYZ Corporation?

Is this the right time to ask for a raise?

Is it important that I attend the annual association meeting next month?

Take a coin and flip it. Heads indicates yes. Tails indicates no. Okay, what was the answer?

Think about how you felt about the answer. Were you disappointed? Relieved? Did you get a thrill of excitement through your body, or a knot of fear in your stomach? Admit it: Did you immediately want to flip the coin two more times and try for best two out of three? (Or have you actually done that already?)

Any of these responses Is an example of your intuition speaking to you. You know the answer. It's the one you wanted in the first place. Your response after you tossed the coin gave you more information about the answer to your question.

So often we expect our intuition to speak like Darth Vader in *Star Wars*, booming out, "Yes! Take that job!" It's more likely that the message will come through subtle feelings, an inner nudge, a physical sensation. When you learn to pay attention to these inner clues and act on them, they can be as loud and clear as any booming voice.

Chapter 19 | When You Need a Creative Decision Fast

The first rule is to pay attention to the intuitive "itches" that accompany certain ideas.

—Charles Best, founder and CEO of DonorsChoose.org

Advertising Hall of Fame luminary Linda Kaplan Thaler is the creative force behind many of the industry's most famous campaigns, including the hilarious Aflac duck, Kodak Moments, and the daring "Yes! Yes! Yes!" for Herbal Essences. Much of her work has become part of the pop-culture landscape, including "I'm a Toys 'R' Us Kid," America's longest-running jingle. She's the co-founder and former CEO of the Kaplan Thaler Group, which she grew from a small startup in her brownstone to a billion-dollar agency working with Procter & Gamble, Pfizer, and Wendy's, to name a few.

The Creative Brainstorming Process

At a recent conference where she was the keynote speaker, she described the creative brainstorming method that launched the award-winning Aflac insurance commercials. Daniel Amos, the CEO of the company, had approached her, saying, "No one remembers our name! We need to make it memorable!" Kaplan Thaler and her staff utilize what she calls the Big Bang. It's an idea that disrupts, has immediate impact, and can't be ignored. "We ourselves had trouble remembering the name," Kaplan Thaler says. "At one of our creative meetings I was repeating the name 'AFLAC, AFLAC' over and over, and one of our brilliant team members reached over and pinched my nose. She said, 'It sounds like a duck quacking.' Everyone thought we were crazy, but I said, 'That's it!'"

In a *USA Today* article from July 2004, Aflac's Amos says brand recognition soared from 13 percent then to 90 percent today: "Everybody had trouble remembering the name. That's why I hired them. It changed our lives. And made my life a lot better."

This same Big Bang approach skyrocketed the then obscure Clairol Herbal Essences into the top-three hair care brands in North America. The creative team was tasked with comparing the shampoo to an orgasmic experience. Many ideas were proposed until Kaplan Thaler said it reminded her of the scene in *When Harry Met Sally*. Meg Ryan and Billy Crystal are sitting in a crowded deli. Ryan's character reveals in embarassingly loud detail how women fake orgasms. The new "Yes! Yes! Yes!" campaign for Clairol Herbal Essences was born.

Though you may not be tasked with equating your product with orgasms, how do you create the Big Bang approach Kaplan Thaler's team utilizes to skyrocket the brands they promote? Whether you describe yourself as a solo-preneur, head of a Fortune 500 company, or somewhere in-between, you're constantly challenged by the issue of how to stand out from the competition. This is why business creativity is a necessity, not a luxury. Are you personally open to new ideas and direction? Do you encourage it in your team and team leaders? You should give this serious thought because your career and your business could depend on it.

Creativity Springs From Intuiton

You need a combination of intuition, creativity, and innovation. All three of these are similar and yet different in important ways. Here's how it looks to me: Intuition is the hunch, flash of insight, or gut feeling that provides the source for creativity. Creativity springs from intuition, which leads to innovation, which, in turn, leads to better, more desirable products and services. Obviously, this can translate directly to the bottom line. So how can organizations be structured and managed so that all three are encouraged and fostered? And what can you do to bring imagination and productivity to your work?

Brainstorming is a term coined by advertising executive Alex Osborn in 1941. He believed that conventional business meetings inhibited the creation of new ideas, and his intention was to design a process that would stimulate originality and spark new ideas. According to Osborn, "Brainstorm means using the brain to storm a creative problem and to do so in commando fashion, each stormer audaciously attacking the same objective." His rules were fairly simple:

No criticism of ideas

Go for large quantities of ideas

Build on each other's ideas

Encourage wild and exaggerated ideas

Osborn found that when he applied these rules to his meetings, new ideas flourished. His staff was no longer inhibited from putting forth ideas that they felt might be considered "wrong" or "stupid." In fact, he encouraged "silly" thinking because it often resulted in a great new ad campaign.

Though the fundamentals of what Osborn considered brainstorming are still with us today, there has been an elaboration of the rules that govern an effective brainstorming session. Following is a description of the basics.

Brainstorming 101

In a quote on AZQuotes.com, Thomas Carlyle seemed to be describing brainstorming when he wrote, "The lightning spark of thought generated in the solitary mind awakens its likeness in another mind." The Merriam-Webster dictionary describes brainstorming as "a group problem-solving technique that involves the spontaneous contribution of ideas from all members of the group." It's an excellent way of developing a number of creative solutions to a problem. It's efficient, too. Ask a question that requires a creative answer. Then gather a group of people and solicit their input. The intent is for the group to come up with as many radical, silly, funny, and off-the wall solutions as possible, as rapidly as they can.

Select Your Team

Begin by choosing a note-taker to record the ideas on large, poster-sized sheets of paper that can be stuck to a bulletin board or along the walls of the room. This will keep all the ideas clearly visible. It's also helpful to use colored pens as an added stimulus to creativity.

The facilitator is the person who writes the statement of intention, gets everything organized, and leads the session itself. If you're the facilitator, your role is to contribute to, but not inhibit, the flow of ideas, and to encourage everyone to participate. Also be prepared with some creativity generators in order to keep the energy crackling and the ideas popping.

Obviously you want to include people familiar with your project, but consider asking staff from different departments to join you. This is a great way to generate some outside-the-box ideas. If appropriate, you could also invite people who are your target audience. If you're trying to come up with ideas for toys, invite kids. If you provide a service to stay-at-home parents, bring them in!

If your group is using brainstorming for the first time, you might send a memo to all participants specifying the time and date along with a brief overview of what to expect. Encourage casual dress. Include the session's focus statement and any additional background information that might be helpful.

Set a Time Limit

There are two schools of thought on the amount of time to set aside for brainstorming. One school says, "No more than 30 minutes!" The other maintains that a good creative session should encompass at least a morning or afternoon in duration. If you choose the longer version, be sure to take frequent breaks to keep minds sharp and creative juices flowing.

Set a Clear Intention

Write a focused, one-sentence question that defines what you want to accomplish. Be specific. If your question is too ambiguous or too general, people won't know where to start. Write this question in big, bold words and post it in a place where everyone can see it.

Here are some examples of good brainstorming questions:

> What events can we sponsor to position our brand as the fashionable walking shoe?

> What are some creative ways we could let business people know about personal chef service?

> How could we make our furniture line more appealing to the luxury market?

> Is there an inexpensive way to communicate that our executive coaching program helps boost corporate creativity?

Dr. Seuss, author of many wonderful children's books, provides this challenge that sounds like a perfect way to begin a brainstorming meeting: "Think left and think right and think low and think high. Oh, the thinks you can think up if only you try!"

Suspend Criticism

All ideas, no matter how crazy they may seem, should be encouraged and recorded without comment or criticism from the group. Roman poet, Ovid, born in 43 BC, proffered this advice, found on BrainyQuote.com: "A new idea is delicate. It can be killed by a sneer or a yawn; it can be stabbed to death by a quip and worried to death by a frown on the right man's brow." I would say this is still true today!

The brainstorming session itself is not the time to evaluate or assess the creative ideas. That comes later. The general goal of brainstorming is to collect as many ideas as possible, making quantity much more important than quality at this initial stage. Philosopher Ludwig Wittgenstein , in the book *Culture and Value*, translated by Peter Winch, suggests we "[d]o not stay in the barren heights of cleverness but descend into the green valleys of silliness." Your goal is to encourage the production of silly, off-the-wall, ridiculous ideas.

Generate Ideas

Here are some other techniques to inspire creativity:

Don't overthink it. Be willing to be silly and outrageous. You're looking to open up the door to the rest of your brain. Just generate ideas quickly in a stream of consciousness.

Try using your non-dominant hand and/or use a medium you don't ordinarily use such as crayons, paint or chalk.

Get a pad of paper and a pen. Set a timer for 10 minutes. Without stopping to think, write your most creative ideas for that period of time.

Imagine that you have more than enough money to accomplish your goals. What will you do?

Think of the opposite: "How could I stop the success of this product or service?"

Ask questions such as "How could we make this product more fun?" and "What would make our product or service unique?"

Fill in the blank: "I wish I had a product that did ____."

If the group is too large, consider having people work in pairs or threesomes and then report back to the main group.

Ayn Fox, founder of the Creativity Lab, coaches individuals and companies in the art of creative thinking. In an interview with her, she adds the following:

Often people reject ideas too soon, or they may go for an idea too quickly. It is useful to evaluate them, no matter how crazy (or wonderful) they may be. She sees it as giving the ideas Tender Loving Care (TLC).

For T— Ask if there is anything tempting or terrific about the idea.

For L— What may be lacking

For C— Is there anything that one can change to resolve what is lacking, so that the idea would be terrific?

When a team is working on a challenge, suggest that individuals "doodle" how they see the problem. No words are allowed. They can either be representative images or abstract doodles. If it's done on one page, suggest they use half the page to illustrate how they see the problem now. On the other half, have them doodle the ideal state of the challenge they are dealing with. Then have them use the doodles to discuss how they see the current and ideal state, and look for similarities and differences.

Encourage the use of metaphor. This can be done in two ways.

#1. They can find a metaphor that explains how they are seeing or feeling about the problem. For example if they are feeling tossed around and overwhelmed, they might say it is like being in a tornado.

#2. Force fit the problem to a random object or experience, something that is in front of them or that comes up in a conversation. Say your stated intention is to come up with solutions to your production problem. You might choose a random object in the room—say a coffee machine—and ask, "How is the production process like making coffee?

After the group has been discussing the challenge, have the facilitator put on some meditation music. Ask participants to pay attention to any imagery that pops up for them. And then force fit the image to the challenge. This is another way to access metaphors.

Using guided imagery, have people close their eyes and imagine a wise person who shares some solutions about the challenge at hand. Have each person write down the insight they receive and then share it in small groups.

There are many creative brainstorming techniques. Figure out which ones work well for you and/or your team. Have fun with those and discard the rest.

Put Your Intuition to Work Tip
A good brainstorming session gives you new ideas, improves your creative thinking, and gives you access to intuitive insight. Give a few of the techniques a try and discover your creative genius at work.

Chapter 20 | Develop an Intuitive Creative Team

Creativity is just connecting things. When you ask creative people how they did something, they feel a little guilty because they didn't really do it, they just saw something. It seemed obvious to them after a while. That's because they were able to connect experiences.

—Steve Jobs

Jan Hills helps leaders and human resources professionals trust their intuition. She runs a consulting business in Surrey, England, called Head Heart + Brain. She acknowledges that the name is pretty quirky, but it says it describes what her company does:

We work with the head—the cognitive, rational content; the heart—the emotional content; and lastly the brain—taking the latest findings from neuroscience to package what we deliver in a way that works for our brain.

We believe through taking this approach that participants and clients will achieve lasting behavioral change.

She explains that during the many years she's worked as a consultant, she's observed, "There are people in every company who always seem to get it right. They make more money for you than most and they're a big reason your company is successful."

She devised a system she calls "The Success Profile" that helps the human resource team understand the secrets of the company's outstanding salespeople. Jan described working with a luxury goods retailer with stores in the United States, Europe, and Asia, and with headquarters in China. She discovered that the sales people with the highest commissions had three distinct characteristics that set them apart from the average salesperson.

They truly cared about the customer, not just making the sale.

They were very goal-oriented. They worked hard, visualized their success, and set high standards for themselves.

If they had a difficult customer, they were able to bounce back quickly by using a positive internal dialogue. In other words, they were able to control their own state of mind.

Jan says:

The human resources group was unusual in that they already highly valued their intuition as a decision-making tool for hiring successful salespeople. My task was to help them develop this skill so they could rely on it as a quick and effective way to hire the right people in an easy and effortless manner.

I prepared for my meeting with them by assembling a set of photographs of a wide variety of individuals along with a description of their backgrounds and biographies. At my training session, I put the photos up on the wall and asked the HR team to write down their impressions of the talents, skills, strengths, and weaknesses of the people in the pictures.

I encouraged them to pay particular attention to how they received this information. Did it come as an image, a feeling, a word or phrase, a physical sensation? I gave them about 30 minutes to complete this exercise.

At the end of that time, we discussed in detail the insights they had perceived about each of the individuals in the photos. When we had completed this part with everyone in the room, I brought out the background/bio pages and read the corresponding descriptions. It was absolutely amazing how accurate they had been!

What's Your First Impression?

Jan notes:

To give you a sense of this, I had thrown in a photo of a very nice looking young man who had, in fact, been convicted of a series of kidnappings. Without knowing anything yet about their colleague's impressions, almost to a person, the individuals had written about this young man things like, "danger," "something wrong," and "dishonest." We were all quite astounded.

The company also created new interview forms that included a space to write intuitive impressions about the job candidate. Jan shared with the group a technique she called "Stop the Clock."

It's basically this:

You're introduced to the candidate and shake hands.

Internally, create a pause and ask, "What's my first impression?"

Jot that down in the space provided on the form.

If the candidate was hired, she encouraged the interviewer to go back to these forms after several months to see if their initial impressions were confirmed. She says, "It was helpful for them to see that their intuitive reactions proved correct in almost all cases. As the result of this training, the recruiters became more confident and the hiring of successful candidates increased proportionally."

What if your company, team, or department is not as open to intuition and creativity as the HR group described? It's tough when there are one or more individuals that resist change, and every company has them. They seem to have an aversion to any modification to the status quo and can be counted on to come up with lines like "That won't work," "It will cost too much," "But, that's not how we've always done it," and, accompanied by a loud sigh, "We *tried* that before." I call them the Creativity Killers.

Is It Creativity or Intuition?

Gail McMeekin, author of *The Twelve Secrets of Highly Creative Women*, explains the difference between intuition and creativity this way, from an interview with me:

Creativity is about bringing something new into being whether it's a new solution to a problem, a new method or device, or a new art form or design.

Intuition is a powerful resource that guides people through the ups and downs of the creative process. Our intuition pulls us towards a specific project or pursuit that will point us in the direction of success.

Put another way, intuition is where your creativity lives. Intuition is guidance within us that provides direction or insight to solve problems, make decisions, and get creative. Creativity is a new way of seeing or doing something that can come about as a result of that intuitive perception.

Creativity and intuition are vitally important to the success of any business. So important, says Dr. John Kao, author of *Jamming: The Art and Discipline of Business Creativity*, "[t]he only kinds of companies that don't need creativity these days are companies that don't need to change." With that said, how do you begin to foster creativity in your own business, team, or department? Here's a list to get you started!

Do Your Research and Then Trust Your Gut

Gary Watson of Adwriter.biz is a freelance copywriter who specializes in writing ads. He's been a creative director at several national and international advertising agencies, and has also won a a number of industsry awards. Here's his take on how to develop a winning creative team:

You first have to gather all the facts. You have to talk to the client and research the product or service. Ideally, you'd talk to the folks who use the product or service and get their take on it. Then you try to put yourself in the place of the "buyer." You're basically trying to answer the question "What is it about the product or service that would create a desire to buy?"

Then you need to look at your own response to what's being offered. What's compelling? What would make you take a look at it? You go home at night and sleep on it. You think about it and live with it, often for several days. You think you're going through these ideas in an orderly manner. However, the best creative ideas tend to come from a chaotic process.

Like many intuitive/creative ideas, the best ones strike when you least expect them—on the train coming home at night, while you're throwing the steak on the grill, or as you drift off to sleep. Creative people don't know where it comes from. They just trust that the ideas will come and open themselves to the process.

In a creative meeting, you have a basic team of creative director, art director, copy writer, and the account executive. You start throwing ideas around. It's often wordplay: It sounds like this or reminds us of that.

Who's going to buy this and what is it about this that will turn them on?

Who are we talking to?

How can we put that out there?

What's the best possible outcome?

The advertising business is fertile ground for intuitive solutions. And the best of them—for example, the Geico gekko—can connect humorously and profitably with millions of appreciative buyers.

Creativity and Intuition Boosters

Would you like some more ideas? Check out the following tips.

Make creativity a core value. Make it clear to your staff that intuition, creativity, and innovation are important to you and the company. Don't just pay lip service to the idea. Back it up with action.

Talk about creativity. How do people define it? Why is it important? What tools does your staff need in order to be creative? What do they need from you as a boss, co-worker, or leader in order to be creative? What encourages creativity? What discourages it?

Design an inspiring work environment. Ask your team to come up with six ways to make the office more conducive to inspired thinking. This could be as simple as painting the office a new color, having imaginative toys on desks, having a bulletin board filled with creative sayings, or allowing for more personalization of individual workstations.

Invest in fun-type training. Employees at Pixar Animation Studios are sent to ballet courses, encouraged to play a musical instrument, trained to juggle. None of these has a direct bearing on people's ability to do their jobs, but it actually makes a huge difference in their ability to bring a creative approach to their work. What could your team do? Take language classes during a coffee break? Participate in an improvisation class? Learn to draw?

Set aside a physical space for creativity. Fill it with crayons, colored pens, big sheets of paper, and craft supplies. Encourage people to use a percentage of their work time to develop new ideas. Put on some great music to encourage the creative juices! Or provide a sanctuary for people who find that inspiration comes to them in a quiet place. Think of it as an "Intuition at Work" room.

Discuss what's working. Many meetings bog down with their focus on problems and challenges. Make sure you devote part of each gathering to a brief discussion celebrating the successes in your office, in your company, or on your staff.

Discuss what didn't work. Often, innovative ideas don't work for one reason or another. Mistakes happen! Advertising icon Leo Burnett put it this way in a meme on BrainyQuotes. com: "To swear off making mistakes is very easy. All you have to do is to swear off having ideas." Rather than ignoring that fact, address it.

Research what others are doing right. Is there another team in your company that is particularly innovative? Talk to them! If you're a solo entrepreneur, consider talking to others in your field. What do they do that works for them? What are their best practices? Look for ways to brainstorm with other individuals or teams.

Create a vehicle for suggestions. Make it known that new ideas are welcome. Post a question of the week that would help stimulate responses. Put it on a bulletin board, a suggestion box, or your company intranet.

Be someone who listens. Creative ideas are often lost when the person in charge doesn't take the time to listen. Make it a priority to listen carefully, elicit opinions, give feedback, and, where appropriate, act on the suggestions.

Have fun! Creative ideas are most easily produced in a light-hearted environment. Start a collection of fun ideas for your company, department, or unit. Ask the staff to suggest ideas for bringing more fun to their work. At least once a week, try one of the ideas. Injecting some fun into your day-to-day operations can be just the tonic to rejuvenate your staff's creativity.

Take frequent breaks. Encourage people to take short breaks, especially when everyone is working on a tight deadline or some other pressure-producing reason. A shift in routine can reinvigorate thought processes. Do something relaxing or silly; go for a walk, grab a latte, or try to solve a puzzle to relieve the tension.

The word *intuition* comes from the Latin, *intueri*, which means "to look within." You have within you and within your team a rich resource. Creative people work from the inside out. They first focus within, and look there for their source of wisdom and inspiration. From that wellspring, brilliant new products, ideas, and businesses are manifested and flourish.

Put Your Intuition to Work Tip
Make it clear to your staff that intuition, creativity, and innovation are important to you and the company. Don't just pay lip service to the idea. Back it up with action.

| | | Put Your Intuition to Work Technique | | |

13 Ways to Inspire Creativity and Intuition in Your Team

Everyone who has ever taken a shower has had an idea. It's the person who gets out of the shower, dries off, and does something about it that makes a difference.

—Nolan Bushnell, founder of Atari

1. Post creative thinking articles on your company intranet, on bulletin boards, in employee newsletters, and in e-mails.

2. Hire people with a broad range of interests and aptitudes. Look for individuals whose hobbies include music, art, or other creative pursuits.

3. Encourage inter-department conversation and meetings. Foster conversation between the creative types and the analytic types. Understand that it takes all kinds to make your company strong.

4. Acknowledge great ideas and innovations on a regular basis through awards, gift certificates, or other form of appreciation.

5. Establish a CCO (chief creative officer) position. One of their duties would be to hold informal lunchtime discussion groups on the topic of creativity and innovation.

6. Establish a quiet room in your company. Encourage employees to use it for individual brainstorming, meditation, or writing.

7. Actively promote the use of intuition by encouraging people to take risks and try new ideas.

8. Make sure at least some of your meetings are nonstructured. Foster brainstorming, a playful approach, and outside-of-the-box thinking.

9. Encourage initiative through suggestion boxes, an open door policy and receptiveness to new ideas.

10. Promote the use of creativity, meditation, and intuition seminars either by paying for employees to go to programs outside the company or by bringing in trainers and consultants on the topic.

11. Buy books on creativity, innovation, and intuition for your senior managers or make them available in a company library.

12. Encourage the development of blogs or online discussion on the topic of creative ideas for your company's services or products.

13. Before your next meeting, ask everyone to contribute a written solution to the problem or challenge you're facing. Begin the meeting by reading the responses aloud. Keep the focus on the solutions, and you'll generate more intuitive responses (and have a constructive and positive meeting!).

Chapter 21 | Liberate Your Inner Innovator

Logic and analysis can always find fault with innovative ideas. Use these tools but use them warily. If your intuition tells you that you have a great idea, then pursue it a little while longer.

—Paul Sloane, author of *The Innovative Leader*

"Companies that master innovation will inherit the future," states Robert B. Tucker, the acclaimed speaker and internationally recognized thought leader in the field of innovation. His seven books, including the latest, *Innovation Is Everybody's Business*, have been translated into more than 20 languages and are used by managers around the world. I interviewed him recently to get his views on the role of intuition in innovation. He says:

Interest in innovation has exploded over the past decade and surveys of CEOs consistently find that it ranks as a top-three priority for 76 percent of chief executives, and 40 percent say it's their top priority. The reasons are clear. Growth is more difficult to come by, yet investors demand it and will go elsewhere if not satisfied with their returns. Survival is tenuous. Just look at Blockbuster, Borders, Blackberry, Kodak, and a host of others who've been forced out of business. The threat of being disrupted—by changing consumer tastes, by new technologies, by demographic trends such as the rise of Millennials—grows with each passing day.

In response, large companies such as GE, 3M, and IBM, are becoming much more systematic and strategic in the way they practice innovation. Up until the past decade, innovation used to be something a company did in fits and starts; it was episodic, often ad hoc and quite heavily dependent on serendipity. If you look at the history of how products came to be, a lot of them were what I call "happy accidents"—Nutrasweet, the microwave oven, Viagra—that created breakthroughs.

In today's hypercompetitive world, organizations can't wait for a happy accident to create their next breakthrough product or service offering. And that's why they are making innovation a strategic imperative, introducing idea management systems so good ideas don't get lost or fail to receive a fair consideration. They're also partnering at a deeper level with customers and strategic partners, and creating risk-taking cultures.

Another thing about the modern practice of innovation is that it has to become a process versus a series of disconnected activities. Some companies say, "Let's improve our new product development process!" or "Let's start an idea campaign" or "Let's change the culture and become more like Google!" What they often fail to understand is that every department in the company needs to be in on generating the ideas. Innovation can't be something that only a very few select people are tasked with doing, while the rest only do execution. It has to be a comprehensive approach because you never know where your next breakthrough idea will come from.

Creativity *helps you come up with ideas.*

Innovation *is the process by which an idea is brought to life.*

Intuition *is an overlay of creativity and innovation. It helps you choose which ideas are the strongest and which decisions will lead to success. It helps you choose partners and collaborators to align with (and which not to!).*

All three are vitally important. In 1986 I researched a book, Winning the Innovation Game, *by going out in the field and interviewing over 50 leading innovators of the day. People such as Dr. Jonas Salk, who discovered the polio vaccine; Fred Smith, the founder of Federal Express; Jackie Sorensen, founder of Aerobic Dancing, and many others.*

What really began to emerge from those conversations was that all these individuals were bringing up intuition, saying they were intuition-driven. They trusted their gut. They used it to read people's motives, they used it to hire people. One entrepreneur told me that he *didn't care if the numbers said he was going to make a jillion dollars (if he made a certain decision), if his gut said danger, he'd walk away and not take the deal.*

Clearly intuition was at the center of their decision-making process. Intuition would help them discover when an opportunity or a problem existed. It could also answer the question of what would dazzle and excite customers if it were brought to market.

I began to call this "informed intuition" because it seems to be the result of accumulated experience in a certain realm, such as business. When you have to make a decision, you still want to immerse yourself in fact-gathering and research first. But frankly, all of this may leave you as confused as before. This is where your gut can help you decide. What I learned from all those interviews, and a career in business coming up on three decades, is that I need to listen to what my gut is trying to tell me.

This is not easy, because of the pace of modern business. With ever-increasing demands on people, most of us have considerably less time for reflection and thinking than we'd like. We're buzzing through our days, responding to over 120 emails, going from meeting to meeting, always trying to be more efficient. We're over-stimulated, overscheduled, over-connected, and overwhelmed. Decisions are made hastily, often while multitasking, and without considering the alternatives.

Whenever I teach classes on innovation strategy, process, and culture—I've had the honor of working with companies in 47 countries—I make it a point to help busy executives and managers avoid the debilitating workstyle that grinds us down and destroys our ability to think original thoughts. I teach them techniques to manage their mental environment, and carve out time for what I call "dream space." It's vitally important. If you've heard me speak, you've probably heard me talk about taking a "Doug Day." This bit of advice comes from an entrepreneur named Doug Green, considered one of the founders of the modern organic movement. When I interviewed Doug at his office in New Hope, Pennsylvania, he explained how once a month, he has an "appointment with me" for a full day. He uses the time not to catch up on e-mail, or even go into the office. He uses it to think. Do we have the right people on the bus? How are we doing against our plan? What trends are gathering momentum that we should be paying attention to? It is on these Doug Days that he tunes in to his intuition.

Intuition can help you read people's true intentions and character, it can alert you to trouble spots, it can help you have an "a-ha" and think up a novel solution to a vexing problem, and it can alert you very quickly when something's not working. The only time intuition will not work is when we tune it out. I always say, when we're needy or when we're greedy, our intuition has no ignition. In other words, if I'm desperate or anxious about something, I seem to override my inner knowing.

Tucker concluded our interview by waxing enthusiastically on the future of business, a subject that holds intense fascination for him as technological innovation increases at an ever-accelerating rate. Will intuition become a quaint, obsolete tool in the digital age? Will Big Data and algorithms dictate our every choice? Will we ask portable super-computers that learn our proclivities and personality styles, and step in to second-guess us at every turn? "Not really," Robert says. "I actually think that intuition will become even more important."

Tap Into Your Own Inner Innovator

How can you put this wealth of information to use and tap into your own inner innovator?

Be curious! Immerse yourself in your topic. Read about it. Talk to others. Do your research. As you're doing this, be aware of what intrigues you, what inspires you to learn more, what compels you forward. Follow that thread. That's your inner innovator leading you in the right direction.

Visualize. What would it look like and feel like if your idea, product, or service were to be successful in the marketplace? Think in both mental as well as emotional images. As you practice this, your intuition will drop clues in your mind about how to most easily achieve your goals.

Be different. Don't do something just because your competitors are doing it. You want to lead the pack. That's what an innovator does! Is there an unusual market you hadn't previously considered?

Think different. Pretend a psychic has predicted your company (product, service, idea) will be wildly successful this year. Grab a notebook and write out a description of exactly how you'll achieve this success. If you're someone who is more motivated by imminent failure, imagine the reverse! The prediction is that you'll fail miserably this year. Write about what got you there. How could you avoid this catastrophe?

Pretend you're the client. Your biggest customer just called and said she was switching to your competitor. Pretend you can read her mind. What are the reasons she's leaving? What compelling case can you make to get her to stay? What innovations are you willing to make as the result of this insight?

Focus on your best/worst decisions. Think back to a time when you made a particularly successful decision or idea. What did it feel like emotionally? How did it feel in your body? How did you know it was a good decision? Do the same exercise with the worst decision you've made. When you're coming up with innovative ideas, pay attention to how they make you feel. This is your intuitive response system in action.

Business 2.0 readers have voted! Your company (idea, product, service) has been voted the most innovative of the year. What are they saying about you? What do you want them to say? What business opportunities would you like this to open up?

Honor your fantasies. (No, not that kind!) If you were to succeed beyond your wildest dreams, what would life look like for you (your team, your company)? Think up some outrageous scenarios. Go for the seemingly impossible! What honors or awards would you receive? Whose recognition would be most important to you? We often limit our ideas of what's possible and therefore drown out the voice of our intuition.

Try on a different persona. Do something different. Take some professional and personal risks. Be courageous! Move out of your proscribed comfort zone. Create a mind's eye picture of yourself as creative, confident, full of ideas, and well-liked. Act as if you're that person. What do you feel like? What ideas can this "new you" come up with?

Tolerate chaos. Innovative solutions don't usually come in a nice, presentable package. They're wild, paradoxical, and unpredictable. They also don't come when you're applying a logical, rational, or structured approach. Learn to be resilient, patient, and willing to keep trying. If one thing doesn't work, the next one might.

Laugh often. Intuition comes most easily to those who have a lighthearted approach to life. I'll close this chapter with a description of a cartoon I saw recently depicting how Sir Isaac Newton came to form the Law of Gravity. Four men are sitting separately in a field. Each one is leaning on a trunk underneath an apple tree and all have writing pads in their hands. Three of the apple trees have moderate size apples hanging on their branches, but the fourth has a huge apple hanging just above the head of the man seated beneath its branches. The caption reads, "Anything yet Newton?

Put Your Intuition to Work Tip

Immerse yourself in your topic. Read about it. Talk to others. Do your research. As you're doing this, be aware of what intrigues you, what inspires you to learn more, what compels you forward. Follow that thread. That's your inner innovator leading you in the right direction.

{ }

Chapter 22 | The Creative Genius Within

The air is full of ideas. They are knocking you in the head all the time. You only have to know what you want, then forget it, and go about your business. Suddenly, the idea will come through. It was there all the time.

—Henry Ford

What do you do when you need an idea and you need it quick? Hire a consultant? Delegate? Panic? No to all of those! You have within you a creative genius ready to help you at a moment's notice. You just need a few suggestions to help prime the pump. As master idea generator Albert Einstein said in a quote on ThinkExist.com, "In the middle of difficulty lies opportunity." Don't lose hope. Help awaits. Just grab a pen and notebook, roll up your sleeves, complete the exercises here, and—voilá—brilliant answers! You had it in you all the time.

Ask the Right Question

What is the biggest challenge you're facing? Phrase it as a question in at least five different ways. For example:

How could we improve employee retention?

What would be the best way to improve employee retention?

Why the heck can't we keep our good people?

Why are people leaving our company in such large numbers?

How can we attract employees who want to stay?

You get the idea. After you've generated your list of questions, circle the one that's most compelling. It will be the one that jumps out at you. Remember when you were in school and the teacher asked a question and you knew the answer? It will make you feel like that. Now, answer the question and come up with a great solution.

Focus on the Solution

You may not know the exact solution to the problem you're facing. However, there are several ways of focusing on the solution. Ask yourself questions like these:

How will I know the problem has been solved?

What will I accept as verification?

How will I feel when my problem is solved?

How will my life (business, team, etc.) be different when this issue is worked out?

What will success look like? If you can begin to focus on the outcome you desire, your intuition will be able to provide you with the most advantageous path to get there.

What would _____do? Fill in the blank with the name of someone you admire. It could be a former or current boss, your neighbor, your mother or father, or a famous historical figure. It doesn't matter who you choose, as long as you view them as possessing the qualities you need to make this decision. Close your eyes and imagine you are this person. How would they approach your issue or problem? Jot down all the ideas that come to you, even if they seem silly, weird, or impossible. Those are usually the best!

Befriend Your Inner Critic

One of the most difficult parts of generating new ideas is that it seems to send your inner critic into high gear. If your inner critic sounds anything like mine, you'll hear such things as "That's a dumb idea," "That won't work," and "Who do you think you are?!" Let me hasten to add that your inner voice (intuition) and your inner critic (IC) have nothing in common. Intuitive messages are usually kind and calming, and make you feel hopeful and optimistic. The IC does the opposite. Artist and poet William Blake is quoted on the Blake Society Website saying, "All great inventions, ideas, businesses and solutions were once simply an idea in someone's mind. What is now proved was once only imagined." In order not to hinder those great ideas, make friends with your inner critic. Tell him or her they have a role in helping you evaluate ideas once you've given them time to develop. Respect your creative process. Let your thoughts percolate for a period of time before you assess them.

Think Like an Alien

If you had just landed on Earth from a planet far, far away you'd constantly be asking who, what, when, where, and especially why. An alien would have very few preconceived notions, so they'd be open to taking in new information. If you were an alien, what would you want to know about this problem? Quoting Einstein from the Think Exist Website again, "If an idea is not at first absurd, there is no hope for it." Write the questions and answers quickly, along with any ideas that are generated. Don't censor anything.

Write a Quick Q&A

Many people have great success gaining intuitive insight by writing a series of questions about their choices. They'll write, for example:

If I hire Mary, will the company's sales increase?

If I hire her, will this be a positive choice?

Will she communicate effectively with her direct reports?

Is she a team player?

What are her strengths?

What are her weaknesses?

When you've completed your questions, write the answers as soon as they come to you. Don't stop in the middle to analyze your responses.

Repeat the process if you have additional issues to consider. The time to evaluate your answers is after you've finished the intuitive portion of the exercise.

Question Your Assumptions

You may be feeling stuck because you're making incorrect assumptions about a person, idea, or situation. Challenge those notions. Ask yourself questions such as "Is there another way of looking at this?" or "What might cause someone to act this way?" The obvious can disguise information that may be critical to understanding your situation. Search for ways to look at the situation differently by changing your perspective. How might you view it from the other person's perspective? If you were an outside observer, how would you describe this situation? Be willing to look at your challenge from a number of different ways. When you find yourself thinking, "Obviously...," question whatever words complete that sentence.

Ask Upside-Down Questions

"The silly question is the first intimation of some totally new development," states British mathematician Alfred North Whitehead on BrainyQuote.com. He would probably agree that if you think about your problem from an entirely different or "upside-down" perspective it may provide some innovative solutions. To use this method, jot down a business challenge you're facing. For example: "We want to increase our sale of widgets in Asia." Now come up with rapid-fire answers to the question "How can we ensure our widgets won't sell in Asia?" Have fun with this! You're looking for outrageous, creative, harebrained, off the wall ideas here. When you're done, choose a few of the more intriguing ones and reverse them (i.e., write the opposite) and evaluate your solutions.

Get Away From the Issue

Many people report that the best ideas come when they're not actively struggling with how to resolve their current issue or challenge! Your brain is too tied up in it. Try something distracting. See a movie, grab a coffee at the local café, take a drive, go for a run, get out among people at a mall, take a walk through your town, read an enjoyable book, do some people-watching at an outdoor restaurant. Once you've distracted yourself for a few hours, come back and try to look at the problem again. You may be surprised by what a few hours of "doing nothing" can provide by way of productive ideas!

Be Open to New Possibilities

Japanese Zen priest Shunryu Suzuki noted in his book, *Zen Mind, Beginner's Mind*, "In the beginner's mind, there are many possibilities; in the expert's mind, there are few." Sometimes all it takes to be open to intuitive insight is to have a beginner's mind: curious, interested, willing, and inquisitive.

Listen to music that is outside your comfort zone. Choose a different route to the office. Drive a little slower. Take a train or bus if you usually drive the car. Try a different kind of ethnic food. If you're usually an extrovert, try being quiet and listening. If you consider yourself shy, practice being confident and extroverted. Try writing the answers to some of the exercises on this page with your opposite hand. Do something creative. Learn to knit. Take a foreign language class. Try a new recipe with a food you've never eaten. Find a new hobby. Read a book on an unfamiliar topic. If you're used to reading dense business tomes, try a murder mystery or a romance novel. Have fun! The purpose of all of this is to give your intuitive mind the message "I am open to new possibilities." It will reward you with rich insight.

Gather Ideas Outside of Your Comfort Zone

Most of us hang out with others who are similar to us. If you're an artistic type, your friends and colleagues are probably fellow creative types (coaches, counselors, marketing people, designers, etc.). An analogous case could be made if you are an engineer, an IT professional, or the like. When you seek advice on a new idea, you're likely to look to your colleagues for feedback. Creative ideas are often sparked by contrasting perspectives. Writer F. Scott Fitzgerald once observed, according to a quote found on AZQuotes.com, that "An artist is someone who can hold two opposing viewpoints and still remain fully functional." Who could you identify that's a little outside your comfort zone to elicit helpful feedback? The fresh perspectives could help to surface new thinking and possibly a fabulous new intuitive idea.

What if Something Good Happens?

I've noticed that clients who are experiencing a major stuck point in their life will negatively predict the possible consequences of their actions and decisions. They get caught in the "If I do Y, what if X happens?" If you do this, you may notice that the end result, the X in this equation is something bad. You tell yourself a story that has an undesirable or scary outcome. You believe the story, you don't want that outcome, no other options appear to exist and you're back in inertia again.

What about telling yourself a different story? Unless you're an incredibly accurate psychic about your own life, who's to say that your bad outcome story is a correct prediction? Be willing to play with some different scenarios. Notice the inner dialogue you have about these various options. They can provide a great deal of insight into what's keeping the creative ideas at bay and allowing you to stay stuck.

Let the Intuitive Muses Provide the Answer

As noted earlier, brilliant answers don't seem to come when you're really focused, intense, and serious. This usually occurs when you need creative insight this very minute. It happens to all of us. You may as well take advantage of this fact and let the muses help you by expanding your options. "Nothing is more dangerous than an idea when it is the only one you have," says philosopher Emile Chartier on a WikiQuote.com page about him.

To begin, choose a topic about which you'd like some fresh insight. Write a line or two about it in your notebook. Then take a 15-minute break and do something routine. If you're home, take a shower, wash the dishes, or pet the cat. If you're at the office, take a walk to the water cooler, have a conversation with a coworker, get a snack from the café or vending machine, or simply take the elevator down to the lobby. When 15 minutes are up, grab your notebook again and jot down all the new ideas you have at the moment. The great thing is that the intuitive muses enjoy helping you. You just have to give them a work assignment!

Whenever you're trying to come up with new ideas, it helps to keep in mind the wonderful dialogue from *Alice in*

Wonderland: Alice laughs and says to the Queen, "There's no use trying. One can't believe impossible things." The Queen replies, "I daresay you haven't had much practice. When I was younger, I always did it for half an hour a day. Why, sometimes I've believed as many as six impossible things before breakfast."

May you believe impossible things and create wonderful possibilities!

Put Your Intuition to Work Tip
We tend to put our focus on what we don't want. Instead, think about the outcome you do want to achieve and then begin to ask your intuition questions, such as "What could I do to increase sales?" and "What are my first impressions of the job candidate?" Keep a journal of your questions and answers. You'll get a confidence boost when you see evidence of the accuracy of your answers.

| | | Put Your Intuition to Work Technique | | |
Tap Into Your Inner Genius

Passion is the genesis of genius.

—Tony Robbins, author and speaker

Masaru Ibuka, founder and chairman of Japan's Sony Corp., was asked in an interview, "What is the secret of your success?" He said he had a ritual. Preceding a business decision, he would drink herbal tea. Before he drank, he asked himself, "Should I make this deal or not?" If the tea gave him indigestion, he wouldn't make the deal. "I trust my gut, and I know how it works," he said. "My mind is not that smart, but my body is." You can read more about that interview in *The Four Desires* by Rod Stryker.

Think of a decision you made recently that you're unequivocally sure was a great choice. Perhaps it resulted in a big sale or customer accolades, or simply gave you great personal satisfaction. Whatever the situation, bring it to mind.

Most likely there were strong logical reasons for making this decision. However, there was probably a strong intuitive reason as well. You want to become familiar with how your intuition conveys a yes response. Spend a few moments checking in with yourself. Here are some questions to ask:

How did you know it was right?

Where did you feel it in your body?

Was there a feeling or emotion that led up to this decision?

If you close your eyes, what image(s) come to mind when you think of this choice?

Was there a word or words you heard in your mind when you were contemplating it?

What made this decision stand out over other options you could have chosen?

How would you know if you were to get this similar "go-ahead" message from your intuition in the future?

You may want to repeat this exercise with a bad choice you made. While possibly more painful to examine, it will nonetheless provide helpful clues about how your intuition communicates to you that you're heading in the wrong direction.

You're the expert on yourself and your intuitive responses. It's as if your inner genius has its own unique language with which it conveys its wisdom. Your job is to be a skilled translator.

Chapter 23 | The Power of Intuitive Selling

Successful salespeople, known as "Heavy Hitters," are experts on human nature who skillfully use language and intuition to build relationships with customers and persuade them to buy.

—Steve Martin, author of *Heavy Hitter Selling*

Before you begin selling your product or service to a prospect, you'll want to get as much factual information as possible. You'll need to do your research. However, this data may not tell you what the client really needs or how to most effectively work with the individual or team. This is where intuition becomes your most valuable research tool.

Successfully making the sale requires that you process hundreds of pieces of information subconsciously. You must develop and trust your ability to use your intuition to read between the lines. Do you press a client for the sale, or do you back off and wait? Are they motivated by the lowest price you can offer, or is the quality of your product or service the prime impetus for buying from you? Many times, logic and analysis will provide that information. On other occasions, your gut feelings or instincts—your intuition—will be the resource you look to for those answers. Richard Whiteley is principal of the Whiteley Group, an international speaking and consulting firm. He co-founded the Forum Corporation and helped build it into a 700-person training and consulting company. Intuition has been an important factor in his success and he shares this knowledge when he speaks on the topic of "Selling Through Service." In an interview, he said:

Using intuition helps a salesperson get off her own agenda and focus on the prospect's or customer's. In sales, you're trained to

*have a call plan. You're instructed to figure out what you're going
to say and what you want your prospect to do as the result of your
plan. Then in a kind of moment of truth, you show up in your
customer's office and execute your plan.*

*Of course, it's wise to have a plan, but if the plan is not deeply
rooted in your customer's or prospect's needs, don't be surprised
when you are informed that your proposal was a well crafted
and nicely presented runner-up! All too often, this gut wrenching
rejection is because the salesperson has not done the front end
work of needs discovery, precisely where using intuition can give
you great leverage. Think of intuition as* a quick and ready insight.
*It is kind of a leap without reasoning or proof. And you will get the
best use of, and greatest return from, using your intuition during the
discovery phase of the sales cycle. This is when the salesperson is
questioning the buyer with the objective of understanding the range
and importance of all his or her needs.*

*It's here, in this give-and-take dialogue, that the salesperson can
earn credibility by making small intuitive leaps that either confirm
the buyer's understanding or, even better, moves the buyer to discover
something important about the product or service that he or she
had not previously considered. When she says, "You know, I never
thought about that." Paydirt! With a statement like that, it is clear
you have just created value for the buyer.*

*If this is so powerful, why don't we use intuition more in our
sales calls? Well, remember back in our call planning? It's amost
like we've done such a nice job planning out the steps we (and
presumably our buyer) will follow, that our behavior is saying we
really don't need the customer to participate at all! If we can just
get him to be quiet and not interrupt our elegant presentation, we'll
be the winner. But the job of the salesperson is not to make the best
sales pitch. It's* to create value in the moment for the person we
are with, whether or not that person is a real or potential buyer,
and whether or not there is a deal on the table to be decided.

*To accomplish this, I tell people to become adept at "full body
listening." You're not just listening to the words. You're listening
to energy, body language, how they greet you, what is not said,*

reactions to others in the room, where they choose to sit, and subtle clues that give you information about their needs and preferences. "Full body" listening will give you intuitive leaps that will enable you to differentiate yourself from others who are chasing the same business as you. It will position you as a "net value creator" in the eyes of your customer, and enable you to create preemptive business proposals and presentations.

Mark has participated in one of Whiteley's training programs. He credits the information as helping him become a national sales leader in his industry. When I asked Mark how he explains his success, he told me that before he meets with a client, he would close his eyes and quiet his thoughts. Then with pen in hand, he would ask his intuition: "What do I need to know about this company or this individual?" He'd jot down all images, feelings, and words as rapidly as they came to him. The answers come to him as he writes. Mark's competition simply scratches their heads in wonder over his results.

Several of the intuitive salespeople I interviewed had a technique similar to Mark's. They might ask questions in their mind before approaching the prospect, or use a more structured method such as closing the door, shutting their eyes, and formally asking their intuition for insight about how best to connect with their customer.

Before You Meet Your Client

A number of the sales pros said they used a variation on the following exercise before ever meeting or talking with a client. There often wasn't an opportunity to read body language, hear someone's voice, and, in some cases, have any conscious knowledge about this person at all, beyond perhaps knowing a name. Somehow they were able to garner significant insight into the prospect without this information. Though this may sound like it's stretching the boundaries of intuition into the psychic realm, try it anyway. If done with an open mind and a little practice, you may find it results in happier clients, increased sales, and ease of negotiation.

To Sell is Human is best-selling author Dan Pink's latest book. He writes about the benefits of positve self-talk ideas that I discussed in the last chapter. Saying things to yourself like "Dan, you've got this! You can do it! You're awesome!" before a sales call creates positive results.

However, his research has found that what he calls "interrogative self-talk" is even more powerful. The question he now asks himself is "Dan, can you do this? And if so, how?" He suggests that questions provoke an active response.

When you ask, "Can you do this?" your brain usually comes up with an affirmative response along the lines of "Yes. I know this client's business. I've got a good product. I'm prepared. I've done my research., etc."

However, "Can you do this?" prompts your brain into truly thinking about and listening for the answer. You might think, "There's a couple things I could do better. Let me correct those things and then I'm confident." You're preparing. You're listening to your intuition. It's a powerful question to add to your postive self-talk toolbox.

Before Your Next Sales Call

Following is an exercise to try before you call on your next client. Set aside at least 15 uninterrupted minutes. Feel free to change the wording or to add your own questions. Write quickly. Don't *think* about the answers.

You may know by now the primary means by which your intuition communicates with you. However, for the purpose of this exercise, pay attention to *all* of the responses that you receive to each question. For example, in response to question #4, you might receive an *image* of customers walking out the door empty handed. (That doesn't need much interpretation!)

The answer you receive to question #5 could be a *knowing* that the company is in serious trouble.

The words *We can increase customer retention* may come to you in response to question #7.

Also be aware of any *physical sensations*. You might ask question #10 and your gut feeling may indicate the answer is no.

Let's begin. Intuitive insight comes most easily when you've closed your eyes, taken some slow, relaxing breaths and centered yourself. Bring the client or company into your mind's eye and focus on them for a few moments.

You may not receive information about every question. If not, skip to the next question. You can come back to it later. If doing an exercise like this is new to you, you may feel like you're making it up. That's okay, too. The proof is in the results. Simply notice and write down everything you're feeling, sensing, hearing, or seeing. Stay open and allow the information to flow without judgment. The time to evaluate the responses will come later.

1. Name of company:
2. Name of prospective client:
3. What do I need to know about this client?
4. What's the biggest problem they're facing?
5. What are the consequences of not solving this problem?
6. How can I (my product or service) help them with this concern?
7. What opportunities are they trying to create?
8. What is the best way to approach this prospect?
9. How can I be most helpful to them beyond the product or service I offer?

10. Do I want to work with this client? If not, why not?

11. Is there anything about the team (company, department) I should be aware of?

12 What should I know about my competition?

13. What can I do to win this account?

Evaluate Your Answers

What do your intuitive responses indicate? Do you now have enough information to allow you to proceed with confidence? It's helpful to keep a notebook specifically for this exercise. The only way to gain confidence is to put into practice the information you've received.

After you've made your sales call, pull out your journal and look at the information you wrote. Use this opportunity to evaluate the intuitive information you had received. Where were you "spot on"? What worked? What didn't work? Were you able to be "present," listening for intuitive insight when you were on the call? Or were you more focused on your sales spiel and forgot to check in?

Was there information you received that doesn't appear to be quite accurate or was outright wrong? That's fine, too. You're practicing developing your intuition. You'll use this information to refine what works and what doesn't. It's not unlike learning to drive a car or to play racquetball. The more you do it, the better you get at it, until it simply becomes second nature.

Of course, this exercise is not meant to replace the normal due diligence required before making a sales call. You'll still want to read their annual report, check out their Website, and read what the media has to say about them. It's just that now, you'll have an additional and much more powerful level of information at your disposal.

You'll notice that much of the focus of the questions in the exercise is about the buyer and their needs. Asking "What's in the sale for me?" won't elicit the response you need to win the account. Legendary speaker and salesman Zig Ziglar states it so eloquently on his Website: "You can get anything in life that you want, if you'll help enough other people get what they want."

Jill Konrath is the author of three bestselling books. Her newest, *Agile Selling*, shows salespeople how to succeed in a constantly changing sales world. In her book, she helps salespeople get their foot in the door and win big contracts in the corporate market. She emphasizes how important it is to "use your brain and think for your prospective and existing customers."

Jill adds: "They're so busy putting out fires, they lack time for problem-solving, strategic thinking, creative alternatives or even reflection. A seller who consistently brings business ideas to the relationship becomes indispensable—winning contracts with minimal competition and at full dollar value."

Intuition helps you understand your customer and provide the creative strategies and insight that Jill alludes to. It's the inner voice that says: "Try this," "Here's the information you need," or "Check this out." Listen to that voice. It's what successful people do.

Put Your Intuition to Work Tip

Before your next sales call, close your eyes, take a slow, deep breath, and ask two questions: "What's the biggest problem this client is facing?" (pause) and "How can my product (service) help them solve this problem?" Tune in via your intuition and listen for the answer.

Chapter 24 | Profile of an Intuitive Sales Pro

A sale is not something you pursue; it's what happens to you while you are immersed in serving your customer.

—Anonymous

Imagine for a moment having a reliable source of information, available anytime you need it, that can tip you off to a prospect's primary buying motivator. Do they want service? No problem. Are they looking for quality? Coming right up. Do they simply want to make a lot of money? You got it.

You don't have to imagine such a scenario. With a little practice, you can become adept at determining how to focus your sales presentation and how best to approach your prospect. Should you be laid back or enthusiastic? Factual or emotional? When you know how to use your intuition, you'll know what it takes to close the sale.

Intuition is the secret weapon of many successful sales leaders. Ask them about it, though, and they're likely to describe it as "gut instinct." Sound familiar? Of course it does, because whether you admit it or not, you're highly likely to have experienced it yourself—and just as likely to have ignored its messages.

The fact is, every salesperson receives intuitive information about how to approach and effectively work with their clients and customers. It's both a gift and a skill, and the more you practice it, the better you get at it. Roy Rowan, author of a study on intuition, said in a 2004 article in BizJournals.com, "This feeling, this little whisper from deep inside your brain, may contain far more information—both facts and impressions—than you're likely to obtain from hours of analyzing data." How do you know when you're tapping into this rich resource? Following is a profile of folks who use it effectively.

Intuitive salespeople:

- See alternatives and possibilities rather than hard and fast rules.
- Sense what's going on in the heart and mind of their client and apply the most effective approach.
- Are able to deal with ambiguous issues.
- Stay focused and neutral in chaotic situations.
- Are adept at reading concealed or unspoken information and raising it to the level of open dialogue.
- Produce win-win solutions to difficult challenges.
- Are able to solve complex problems where data is often incomplete.
- Are practiced at creating a sense of high motivation for themselves and others.
- Foresee problems and set about solving them before a crisis emerges.
- Are adaptable to a wide variety of cultures, diversity, and belief systems.
- Focus on similarities and connection, not differences.
- Listen deeply to others' needs, wants, and desires.

After looking at the list, you'll probably feel even more inspired to learn how to use and expand the valuable inner resource of your intuition to succeed in sales. Here are some tips from the intuitive sales pros I interviewed.

Keep Your "Inner Salesperson" Positive

Pay attention to what you tell yourself about your sales prospects and your life. If your "self-talk" is positive and optimistic, your personal and business life will reflect that. Try a simple experiment. Close your eyes and say the following to yourself for about 30 seconds: "I'll never get ahead. I'm not good at sales. I won't make my quota this month." How do you feel? Depressed? Demoralized? Hopeless?

Now do the same experiment and focus on these statements:

Things have a way of working out.

I'm learning some new skills and things are beginning to change for me.

Today I'll take steps that will open up opportunities for more income.

I have a great product and I enjoy letting people know about it.

Now how do you feel? Hopeful? Optimistic? More confident? When you're in this state, it's much easier for you to be open to intuitive messages pointing you to avenues of increased prosperity.

Use the Power of Silence

As any good salesperson will tell you, sometimes the best thing to do is shut up. But there are times when you also need to silence your mind to receive valuable intuitive insight. When you need help making a decision—pause—take a deep breath, reflect on the question, and allow the intuitive impressions to come to you. Intuition is often described as "still and quiet." It doesn't shout out the answer. It is much more subtle. You may, in fact, feel like you're making up the answer. The truth about the wisdom you receive will only be known when you act on the information. If your workplace doesn't lend itself to quiet reflection, get out of the office and take a walk or take a seat in your car.

Pay Attention to Your Energy

If a sales strategy or decision leaves you feeling drained or bored, that's a clear message from your inner guidance saying "This won't work" or "Try something new and different." Conversely, if you feel energized and enthusiastic, your intuition is giving you the green light to continue with your plan of action.

Build Some Downtime Into Your Daily Schedule

It might make logical sense to pack sales calls into every moment in order to make efficient use of your workday, but not for the intuitive sales pros. They value having a breathing space. They use it for reflection, daydreaming and thinking. One person said, "I've lost more sales when I'm overwhelmed and stressed. When I build some downtime into my schedule, I'm relaxed and things happen effortlessly. I catch people at just the right time. Opportunities come my way without me chasing after them. It's like I'm a sales magnet when I'm in the flow!"

Envision Your Success

Spend time each day imagining your ideal work life. What does success look like? What does it feel like? Imagine you are living it now. What are you wearing? What are you feeling? Who are the people around you? We are often quite clear about what we *don't* want. The path to success comes from spending time thinking about what you *do* want. What does an ideal day, month, or year look like to you? Being clear about what you want is often the first step in being able to create it. Successful people visualize their goals and dreams. Your intuition can help you achieve success when you know what you want to achieve.

Pay Attention to the Message You're Sending

John Assaraf has built four multi-million-dollar businesses and now mentors entrepreneurs through his company, One Coach. In his sales trainings, he advises students to watch their inner dialogue. When I interviewed him, he stated, "If your thoughts are on 'I have to make this sale in order to pay my mortgage or make my car payment' your energy is in the wrong place. Your client will pick up on it immediately." Instead, he recommends they stay focused on the qualities of kindness, honesty, caring, authenticity, and doing the right thing for the individual. "You want the client to feel good about you and about doing business with you. This attitude may not result in an immediate sale, but it pays off in the long run," he said.

Create a Definition of Your Perfect Customer

Let's face it: It's no fun working with people you don't like. You probably spend a lot of time with your clients. No one looks forward to hanging out with people who are cranky, difficult, and demanding. Turn the tables! Identify the qualities of those you've most enjoyed working with, currently or in the past, and begin to magnetize more of the same.

Stacey Hall and Jan Brognicz are experts on this topic and the authors of *Attracting Perfect Customers*. They suggest you stop *looking* for your perfect customers and *attract* them instead. Sound too good to be true? They believe a "perfect customer" list is an important part of the strategy to easily and effortlessly attract those clients.

How would you describe them? Do they have a good sense of humor? Perhaps they simply pay their bills on time. You may enjoy working with them because they appreciate you and your hard work. Possibly you like them because you and they have similar values. Whatever your reasons, create a written list of the attributes and characteristics of that perfect customer.

This list will "prime the pump" of your intuitive mind, so next time you're on a sales call, remember your list. Ask your intuition, "Does this person or company match my perfect customer profile?" If you feel excited, pleased, and energized by the thought of working with them, pay attention! Your intuition has just served up an affirmative answer!

Take the Time and Make the Sale

Be sure to set aside time to routinely check in with your intuition. It won't be long before you'll be experiencing faster, stronger, and more accurate insights. Though intuition can be described as a secret weapon, there's no big secret about how to use it. Follow the suggestions I've outlined in here, and the more specific techniques in the next chapter, and begin to reap the rewards of this powerful competitive advantage.

Put Your Intuition to Work Tip
There are times when you need to silence your mind to receive valuable intuitive insight. When you need help making a decision—pause—take a deep breath, reflect on the question, and allow the intuitive impressions to come to you.

Chapter 25 | 8 Ways Intuitive People Think Differently

Learning to trust your instincts, using your intuitive sense of what's best for you, is paramount for any lasting success. I've trusted the still, small voice of intuition my entire life. And the only time I've made mistakes is when I didn't listen.

—Oprah Winfrey, talk show host, actress, and philanthropist

As you've read so far in this book, intuition provides much more than just quick answers to a problem. It's also a mindset for how to approach life and the inevitable life changes and challenges. Intuitive people think different! This chapter contains eight attitudes they adopt, with examples.

1: They Set a Clear Intention

Intuition is our inner GPS. When you're clear where you want to end up, your inner guidance can do a great job of getting you there.

Tracy is the chief product officer for a women's clothing company. She says:

I always try to define the outcome I want. It may be something intangible, like I want to come away from a conversation with a staff member with both of us feeling positive about the interaction.

A more tangible example would be for a meeting like I held with my team this morning. I wanted to come up with three winning prototypes for a new line of women's dress pants. I state my intention at the beginning of the meeting and encourage others to do the same.

I find that kind of clarity allows creative ideas to flow unimpeded. We stay much more attentive. The meeting is positive because we're focused on the result we want rather than getting distracted by complaining or getting sidetracked by what's not working.

2: They Listen Carefully to Others

Whether it's empathizing with a co-worker or listening to a client discuss their product needs, intuitive people listen differently.

Sharon is a freelance public relations specialist who says:

I'm often in a situation where I have to get up to speed very quickly. My client may be experiencing a crisis and need my PR expertise to manage it. Or, more likely, it's a new business where the owner wants some positive media attention. Either way, my skill at intuitive listening helps me home in on what the client needs and where I can best focus my efforts.

I try to listen compassionately with an open heart. This means not judging their words or experience. I put myself in their shoes. What would I need or want in this situation? I also pay attention to what they say that has energy or enthusiasm and what doesn't. It may sound a little complicated as I describe it. Perhaps it's best summed up with the idea that I hold the question "What does this person need and how can I help?" in my mind as we have the conversation. My intuition is then on the alert and sends me the right answers.

3: They're More Patient

Not everything happens immediately even when you use your intuition! Jerry, who has had a successful marketing business for the past 20 years, says:

I used to be a very Type A kind of guy. I would pound the pavement trying to drum up new clients, going to every networking meeting I could find. I was burning out fast.

I had a minor heart attack at about year 10 of my business. I was only forty. It was a total wake up call that said to me that I needed to pay attention to the quality of my life. I learned to slow down and be more deliberate. I would begin my day by asking myself "What do I want to accomplish?" and "What's the best way to proceed?" I would close my eyes and just try to get a sense of the direction to focus my day.

I kept a pad of paper beside me and jotted down any ideas, notes, "a-ha" moments. Interestingly, since I began this practice, business and life in general feels more effortless. I don't think I'd like my clients to hear this, but I feel like I'm partnering with a Higher Intelligence that wants to help me. I've learned it doesn't have to be hard! I just need to be patient and let it come through.

4: They Ask the Right Questions

"What's wrong with me?" "Why is business at a total standstill?" "Why can't I hire good employees?" These are not helpful questions if you want helpful intuitive answers.

Jean is a sales rep for a rapidly growing cosmetics line. She gets paid on commission through sales to drug store chains, beauty supply stores, department stores, and the like. According to Jean:

I've always enjoyed sales, and the beauty industry is one that I find fun and exciting. My current company hired me three years ago. I was the top salesperson in my previous job, so my new boss had high expectations of me.

For some reason, I couldn't seem to hit the ground running and fell into a kind of funk. I was unfavorably comparing myself to others. I started to convince myself I didn't have what it took to succeed. It was during that time that I read your book, Divine Intuition. *You had a chapter on positive self-talk. I realized I needed to refocus on what made me successful previously because now I was focusing on all that I was doing wrong.*

I began asking myself questions like "What could I do to win this account?" "What are my strengths?" and "What's the best way to approach this person?" When I started listening to the answers, my self-confidence improved along with my sales. It seems somewhat magical, but it's all on where I put my attention. Do I focus on my weaknesses or on the success I want to achieve?

5: They Have Personal Tools for Inspiration

Intuitive people seek and use tools for encouragement and motivation.

Some sort of daily reading was mentioned by almost everyone in my research and interviews of intuitive people. The Bible or other religious text was mentioned frequently. The reading might come in the form of an inspirational daily message via the Internet or from short passages from a book they were reading.

Meditation and guided imagery were the second most mentioned inspiration tools. Kelly Howell's BrainSync.com site and her app Meditate.me were popular. The two other apps with a high number of happy listeners were Simply Being and Omvana. The guided meditations for stress relief and another for healthy sleep by Belleruth Naparstak at HealthJourneys.com also had a lot of fans.

Jen, a Yoga Teacher with a thriving suburban practice, says:

I use the tools of meditation and inspirational reading to keep me sane and focused throughout the day. Each morning, I choose a quality I want to embody. Today it was "compassion." Yesterday my morning reading was about "centeredness." I try to view all interactions that day through that lens. When I do this, I find that I'm much more in the flow. I believe that business ideas, positive exchanges and interesting synchronicities happen with increasing frequency as the result of this practice.

6: They Have Coping Strategies for Major Life Transitions

Intuitive people understand that life events such as divorce, health challenges, and business failures can happen to all of us. Instead of resisting the experience, they think about how to reinvent themselves.

Harry describes his former self as a "hard-charging jerk" in business. He'd prefer not to talk about his previous occupation because:

I saw everyone and everything as my competition and made a lot of enemies through my behavior.

I got virtually knocked to the ground a few years ago by a divorce and a cancer diagnosis that happened at the same time. I was really dependent for a while on the kindness of a couple of friends who saw me through the worst of the situation. I had a few months where I wasn't able to get out of bed and it gave me a lot of time to think.

I knew that I couldn't keep going in the same direction any longer. I decided to go on a week-long retreat. I learned to meditate. I started to eat healthy food. I saw a counselor. I had many intuitive sessions with Lynn. I chose to see this as a period of time to reinvent myself. I had to trust that there was something I was supposed to do on the other side of this crisis. That was hard for me. I really feel like a different person now. I'm a lot kinder and more patient. I've started volunteering with a veterans group and it's given me a purpose to my life that didn't exist before.

7: They Get Answers in Their Sleep

"Enough" sleep is often a relative number, but many reported it as important to their creativity and inspiration.

Elaine works in the high-tech industry. She tells me that she's often hyper-focused on her work:

I've got a very perfectionist personality. It makes it a little difficult to find intuitive answers during the day. It's like there's an "inner censor" in my brain that is always judging my performance. It also seems to like logical answers. The best way for me to come up with creative ideas is either through taking a nap at my desk at work or when I awaken in the morning after a good sleep.

Before I come fully awake, I ask myself "What wisdom has my sleep delivered?" I jot down any dreams, dream fragments or words and phrases running through my mind. About 70 percent of the time there's a great pop of insight that I can apply to a project that I'm working on.

8: They Feel Inspired by a Larger Calling

Many people reported going through a major life change where what they were doing no longer felt purposeful. Intuition was a key factor in finding meaning again.

Ann had been a nurse for 20 years. She says:

The majority of the time I worked as a medical surgery nurse in an ambulatory care unit. It was stressful but engaging work. However, after I discovered I had breast cancer, my world turned upside down. I spent the better part of a year being partly out of work on disability dealing with chemotherapy, radiation, and physical therapy. When it was time to return to full-time, I found I just couldn't do it. My heart was no longer in it.

This presented a big crisis for me. My whole identity had been wrapped up in being a nurse and caring for people. I spent a few months feeling quite depressed, until a counselor I worked with suggested I try to see this situation as an open door to an opportunity for something new and positive. That gave me a much-needed perspective change.

I began to realize that so many other people who had gone through a life-changing event, like cancer, felt adrift like me. When I thought about helping those survivors navigate this transition, I began to feel excited. I took that as a clue from my intuition. I enrolled in a nurse coaching certification program. After completing the curriculum, I decided to hang out my shingle as a coach. I now support women all over the country by phone in my home office. I help them trust their own intuition, find their way back "home" to their own calling, and get through any of the aftermath of their diagnosis and treatment. I love what I do. It's as if my own dark time and cancer diagnosis led me to this work.

Put Your Intuition to Work Tip

After reading this chapter, which of the eight ideas speaks to you most strongly? What could you do to incorporate it into your life?

| | | Put Your Intuition to Work Technique | | |
Put Your Intuition to Work Checklist

Intuition is one of the most important abilities we can cultivate. . . It is becoming necessary for a comprehensive personal and global perspective.

—Jagdish Parikh, co-founder of the World Business Academy

You've got a big decision to make. Here's a checklist of the top-12 ideas to use that will allow you to quickly access your intuitive insights.

1. State your desired outcome. It can be as general as "Motivate my sales team" or as specific as "I want to partner with the Smith Company."

2. If you have time, immerse yourself in information about your subject.

3. Use your logical mind to analyze the options available to you and then give it over to your intuition to make the best choice.

4. Ask your intuition a question: "What should I do about...?"; "How can I...?"; and "What do I need to know about...?" are all good examples of ways to phrase a question to evoke intuitive information.

5. Take a break. Get away from your desk and preferably out of the office for at least five minutes.

6. Quiet your mind with a breathing exercise or a simple meditation. Clear your mind of distractions. Listen for the answers.

7. Make a hypothetical choice. Does it feel right in your gut? Do you feel energized by the decision? Can you see the successful completion of this plan of action. If the answer is yes to all, you're on the right track. If not, choose again.

8. Close your eyes and ask for an image or symbolic picture that represents the answer.

9. Take out your notebook or laptop and brainstorm a number of possible options. At the end of 10 minutes, go through your list. Which of the choices feel best to you?

10. Let go of the "what ifs." It's possible to endlessly obsess over possible consequences of your decisions until it clouds intuitive vision.

11. What do you know for sure? What pops into your mind when you ask that question?

12. Go with what you know. Take a bold step and then another! Keep tuning into your intuition and asking questions each step along the way.

My prediction? You're going to continue on the path to success by trusting your gut and growing your business!

Chapter 26 | I Should Have Trusted My Gut!

It's imperative to listen to your intuition because you can head a
blossoming crisis off at the pass. You have to figure out how intuitive
impulses feel to you and allow it to become your partner in your success.
It will never lead you astray.

—Robert Tucker, author and innovation expert

One of the questions I'm frequently asked is "If you're so intuitive, why haven't you ever won the lottery?" The answer is I did (sort of). A few months after I was married, I woke up early one Wednesday morning with six numbers running through my head. I found I could neither fall back to sleep nor stop the numbers from endlessly repeating themselves in my mind.

I had never played a lottery before, but it occurred to me that these numbers might represent a lottery win. My husband, Gary, was snoring beside me. I shook him gently and said, "How many numbers are in the Massachusetts State Lottery?"

"Six," came his mumbled response.

"I think I might have the winning lottery number," I replied.

He was on his feet, grabbed a paper and pen, and was ready to write down the numbers before I barely had them out of my mouth. I'd never seen him move that fast!

With the "winning numbers" in hand, Gary said he'd play them in the Wednesday lottery. I promptly put the whole thing out of my mind until Friday morning when I casually asked over breakfast if he'd checked on whether our number had won.

He confessed that he'd had a crisis at work and had forgotten to play the game on Wednesday, but hastened to add that he had placed bets for both Thursday and Friday.

We took out the newspaper to find the lottery list. You guessed it: My numbers were the winning numbers for *5.2 million dollars* on Wednesday—the day I received the information and the day he *didn't* play it.

Sigh... So close and yet so far away. And, yes, I'm still married to him.

The Disappearing Social Media Consultant

My client Janet described a "should have trusted my gut" story during one of our sessions. She had just started her Internet marketing business and had met with some early success. She was very excited and more than a little overwhelmed by all the details. The learning curve was steep:

I met a woman at a networking meeting who seemed to offer just the set of skills I was lacking. She was a website designer who had a savvy team of social media folks at the ready to work on any project I sent her way. She also spoke about how her many clients could use my services. She was incredibly charming, great at sales, and very persuasive. Any concern I voiced was met with a positive "can do" response. I was eager to begin working with her because I believed it would help my own small business become profitable much more quickly.

In retrospect, I realize that I was too eager. *That should have been my first clue. I ignored the caution signs that my intuition was firing off. Things happened so fast that I disregarded or explained away situations like missed deadlines, unmet expectations, billing errors, and poor communication. I would get an upset stomach when I had to talk with her. She kept trying to convince me that I was at fault. The worst part was that I believed her! I kept telling myself that I just had to be patient as we worked out this new business relationship.*

About five months into working together, I got a call from one of my clients. He had been with me from the beginning and was a long-time colleague who I trusted. He started the conversation

*by stating bluntly: "You are losing your business to this woman."
He then provided details about how she was going behind my
back and trying to convince my clients to only work with her by
undercutting my fees.*

*I was incredibly distraught. I did some investigation and found
that what he said was true. I developed some backbone, hired a
lawyer, and severed the relationship with her immediately. I had a
lot of relationship repair to do with my clients. It cost me money,
my reputation, and a great deal of stress.*

*I see now that the decision to work with this woman was a
combination of not having confidence in myself, being too eager or
excited, and being overly busy. They all added up to not trusting my
gut.*

*When I recall my initial conversation with her, my head was
saying, "Yes! Yes!" and all other signs were saying, "Run in the
other direction!" But in the end, I emerged stronger, wiser, and
with a determination to firmly trust my intuition in all endeavors.
It was an expensive lesson to learn and it's served me well in the
many years since it happened.*

If you're honest with yourself, you've done it too. It's those
times you said, "I should have trusted my gut. I knew something was wrong with _____ and I went ahead anyway."
Maybe you didn't do it as dramatically as Janet and I did, but
it's important to pay attention to those lapses because they can
teach you just as much as the times that you trusted your intuition and things worked out. Let's take a walk down Memory
Lane and see if we can jog some of those recollections.

Confess! You've Done it Too!

Name someone you shouldn't have trusted, but did anyway. What were the signs? How did you know?

Describe a time you listened to someone else's advice and
ignored your own inner wisdom.

When did you have a strong inner message to walk away from something and instead headed toward it?

When did you "just know" something, but allowed logic or reason to steer you in the wrong direction?

Have you ever said, "I just knew that would happen!"? What did you know and how did you know it?

Have you ever hired someone because their references checked out even though you had a strong feeling they weren't right for the job? What do you wish you had done differently?

Describe a time when you knew you were off track either personally or professionally. What were the indications of this and what do you wish you'd done differently?

Your boss (company, partner) were going in a direction you knew wouldn't work. What did you say? What could you have said or done differently?

The analysis and research all pointed in one direction. You knew in your gut that success lay in the opposite route. How do you wish you had responded?

You chose a job that you knew you shouldn't take. How did you know that and what happened?

You had an odd feeling in your gut, an inkling, a foreboding. Something told you to "stay away" from this person or situation. What happened when you allowed your logic to override your intuition?

How has not trusting your gut hurt you professionally, personally, financially, or even physically?

It takes courage to tune into your intuition and also to pay attention to what it's telling you. However, like any skill or ability, the more you practice it and take action, the better you get at it. Ultimately, you have a reliable radar that keeps you out of danger and away from anything that would derail your success or put you in harm's way.

Pay Attention to the Early Warning Signs

That's what happened to Manny, who trusted his gut—and it may have saved his life. Manny says:

I travel a lot on business. I'm a consultant in my industry and I'm often called upon to be a speaker on my topic at various international conferences and conventions. Several years ago, I had the opportunity to speak at one of these events. I was eager to go, as it was something I wanted to attend, and it represented a major professional achievement to be invited as a speaker.

The first clue that I ignored from my intuition was that I kept procrastinating making the travel arrangements. I've learned that when I consistently put something off, there's a message there. I shouldn't ignore it! However, the deadline was fast approaching and I didn't heed the message my gut was sending. I made the flight and hotel reservations.

As the date approached, I began to get inexplicably anxious. Again, I travel and speak a lot so it wasn't about that. I couldn't put my finger on it. I was busy and I didn't take the time to sit with this unusual feeling and understand what it was trying to communicate. Missed opportunity number two!

On the day of the flight, I got to the airline ticket counter only to discover I had the wrong flight time. I barely made it aboard the plane. I got there just as they were calling for final boarding. Once again, highly unusual for me! I don't think I had ever done that before and it worried me. Missed intuition opportunity number three.

Finally, I was at my destination. I had gotten there a day early to shake off jet lag and walk around the city. My talk was during the morning of the next day. I slept fitfully that night despite being dead tired. I kept having weird and unusual dreams about being in danger. This definitely put me on the alert. The only other time I had had those strange dreams was just before my dad died in a car accident. I'll call this dream an "almost missed" intuition message. I was definitely feeling cautious and more aware of my surroundings at this point.

My speech went great and I was pleased and relieved, but oddly, still very anxious. I had requests for a lunch meeting from several prospective clients who had heard my talk. I wanted to connect with them but found I desperately wanted to get out of the hotel. I suggested a local restaurant in the area that I had discovered during my walk the previous day. They were puzzled about the change in location, but agreed.

I sealed a really great deal during our lunch conversation. We lingered over repeated cups of coffee at my behest. I selfishly wasn't looking forward to getting back to the conference. Finally, it was time to leave and we grabbed a cab back to the hotel. When we arrived it was surrounded by police and ambulances with sirens wailing and lights flashing.

It turned out that there had been a shooting just outside our conference room. All of the attendees were still in there behind locked doors fearing for their lives. Eventually, we found out that no one from our group was either involved nor was anyone physically hurt. However, the anxiety and fear they lived through for several hours was something that will probably stay with them forever.

I'm very grateful that my intuition warned me away. I wish that when I get these messages they were more direct. "There will be a shooting. Stay away during these time periods!" It just doesn't work that way. So I'm left with profound appreciation that I have an early warning system even if it doesn't provide specifics. I have learned to pay attention.

Manny went on to share his favorite technique when he gets one of his "intuition early warning signs." He takes some time out from his day, usually just a few minutes. He shuts the door, turns off his phone, and computer and gets quiet. He asks, "What does my intuition want me to know right now." He listens and acts on the answer he receives. Listening may have saved his life.

Put Your Intuition to Work Tip

Think back to those times when you "should have trusted" your intuition and, sure enough, things went awry. It's important to remember them because they can teach you just as much as the times that you trusted your intuition and things worked out well.

{ }

| | | Put Your Intuition to Work Technique | | |
Listen to Your Gut—Literally

There are times in all of our lives when a reliance on gut or intuition just seems more appropriate—when a particular course of action just feels right. And interestingly, I've discovered it's in facing life's most important decisions that intuition seems the most indispensable to getting it right.

—Tim Cook, Apple Computer

Did you know there are neurotransmitters in your gut? They're the brain chemicals that communicate information throughout our brain and body. They relay signals between nerve cells called "neurons." The brain uses neurotransmitters to tell your heart to beat, your lungs to breathe, and your stomach to digest. They also can inform you when you're about to make a good or bad decision.

To do this, think of a decision you need to make. For the sake of this exercise make a hypothetical choice. Let's say your decision is "I will hire the Win New Business PR Consultants."

Say the decision out loud: "I will hire the Win New Business PR Consultants."

Notice the physical sensations in that area and ask yourself how this decision makes you feel.

Do you feel constricted, tight, or nauseated?

Or do you feel the opposite—open, comfortable, and at ease?

Also pay attention to your general energy level when making this decision. A good decision will make you feel open, energized, and expansive. A bad decision will generally make you feel shut down, drained, and devoid of energy.

Still having difficulty identifying your feelings?

Think of a negative situation from your past. An example might be getting fired from a job, or simply the memory of someone you strongly disliked. Recall this moment or person. How does your stomach feel? Did your heart race? Do you feel generally tight and uncomfortable? That's your body telling you to stay away from a person or situation.

Next, pick an image of something or someone you love. This could be your spouse, your kids, your pet, or even a hobby you enjoy. What is your body communicating as you bring this person or situation to mind? Generally people report openness, energy, and expansion. Those are the feelings and impressions to look for when you're moving in the right direction.

Many of us discount those physical and emotional impressions. Pay attention to yours! Explore them further. They hold the clues to your intuitive wisdom.

Chapter 27 | When *Not* to Trust Your Gut

My intuition never fails me. It is I who fail when I do not listen to it.

—Hazrat Inayat Khan,
Sufi mystic

Joe's business was slowly failing and he knew it. The competition was ramping up. They were promising newer, faster, and easier ways to offer the home health medical device products that his family-owned company had provided for decades. He had asked for recommended courses of action from his sales, marketing, and accounting department heads. He sat down to read the completed reports on a Sunday morning over coffee.

When he read the sales and accounting proposals, he become more confused and uncertain. Sales had recommended an increase in staff. Accounting had strongly recommended a decrease in personnel with recommendations for layoffs. He got excited when he read the marketing department idea. They had suggested they begin promoting Joe and his business to the local media.

Joe will admit that he has a very healthy ego. The idea of being interviewed on television and written about in the media appealed to his vanity. He says, "I will show my competitors who the victor is!" He felt excited and determined that this was his intuition speaking. He hired a PR team who got him a number of good local media placements. The problem quickly became obvious. Instead of focusing on his business and its value proposition in the local market, he simply chose to rail against his competition.

Intuition Lesson #1: Be Clear About the Outcome You Want

It would have been more fruitful for Joe to sit with the various proposals from his team, asking something along the lines of "What should we do to successfully grow our business?"

Charlie had an issue that at first seemed similar to Joe's. Despite a lot of outward success, his business seemed to be losing money month after month. He became convinced that one of his sales team, who he didn't like, was stealing from him. Believing that this was a message from his intuition, he fired him. Unfortunately for the salesperson and for Charlie, this didn't solve the problem. Charlie kept looking at people in his organization who he felt didn't perform according to his standards or weren't respectful to him. Several more employees were forced out due to his inaccurate intuition. Finally, the head of his accounting department came to him with hard evidence. Indeed, there was embezzling going on. It turned out to be Charlie's much-adored office manager. She had created a separate account and was siphoning off more and more money each month.

Intuition Lesson #2: Don't Let Your Feelings Be Your Only Barometer

Charlie made decisions that were often impulsive and thoughtless. He had an "off with their heads" mentality if he believed someone wasn't living up to his standards. This, in part, was his definition of intuition. If it felt wrong, it was. No questions asked. It was a hard lesson for him to learn. He lost key people and didn't recognize the embezzler because she was "so nice" according to him. Logic and research are often helpful partners in trusting your intuition.

"We've tried this before and it didn't work" was Susan's first response when she heard the suggestion from her marketing team. She was the CEO of a technology company and listening to the recommendations of several key staff who were hoping to make inroads with a current client. The client wanted the software her company produced to be customized for their large company.

Susan felt that saying no to this request was both logically prudent and a strong intuitive message. After all, a similar company had wanted customized advanced features a few years ago. It had taken a lot of employee time and other resources and hadn't resulted in an increase in sales. She had a good relationship with the company making the current request and believed that the goodwill would be enough for this company to overlook the denial of customization. She was wrong. The client went to a competitor.

Intuition Lesson #3: The Past Is Not a Preview of the Future

Successful intuitive decisions are in part made up from pattern recognition. "X happened before and Y was the result." You may be tempted as Susan was to repeat the same equation and come to the same conclusion. However, if you try to squeeze a current situation into an old pattern, you might miss some of the complexity and change that's taken place. What could Susan have done differently? She could have done more research as well as gained more insight into what had changed in the marketplace. She based her decision on some old history and decisions that were no longer current.

Martin is a client who called me excited about a new business opportunity. He'd been working as a leadership coach for a few years and, though moderately successful, he had dreams of a much larger income and more opportunities. He described a new wellness company that sold vitamins, supplements, and high-nutrition shakes. It was a multi-level-marketing concept and he was being invited to participate at a high level. He tried the products, felt he had some improvement in his energy, and was excited to buy in.

The founder of the wellness company was an incredibly charismatic guy who held a series of video conferences with those wanting to buy into the opportunity. The total initial investment was $5,000 worth of products, membership, and administrative costs. That sounded like a reasonable sum to Martin, who was persuaded that he could rapidly make that amount back within a month or so by following the founder's persuasive model.

Martin was incredibly eager and enthusiastic to make this work, so much so that he invested more money to attend an in-person conference in order to meet the founder. There he heard a lot of hype and talk of easy money, and met gung-ho converts who were relatively new to the business. He also realized that many of the people who had made money were what he called "FOF": friends of the founder, who had gotten in on the ground floor and made a lot of money off of the down-lines they had created. Disillusionment set in fairly quickly as Martin tried to sell the products to his friends and clients. He soon realized it required a certain kind of personality and a large group of wealthy, health-oriented acquaintances to succeed. He lost a few thousand dollars as well as his trust in his intuition.

Intuition Lesson #4: When You Are Too Excited About a Decision, *Slow Down*

In retrospect, Martin recognized that much of his decision to participate in this company was based on the charisma of the founder. He described feeling over-eager to the point of not listening to his wife's and friends' entreaties to stop and think through this decision. As a side note to this bad decision, he realized it wasn't in keeping with this self-described life purpose to counsel and coach. It was a lesson learned. He still enjoys and benefits from the product, just not from selling it as a business endeavor!

Why Do People Make Bad Decisions?

You're Lazy!

All good decisions are a mix of logic, facts, some research, subconscious and conscious knowledge, as well as intuition. If you're a lazy person, it's all too easy to lean back in your office chair and simply state, "My gut says_____" and leave it at that.

You're Too Rushed

You've got a deadline to meet and a big decision to make. Your mind is going in 10 different directions all at once. Multi-tasking is not your forte, but you haven't got time to do any background research for this upcoming decision. You simply wing it and call it your intuition. You hope no one notices.

You Haven't Considered the Consequences

Research shows that if you can actually slow down and consider various possible outcomes, you'll make a better decision. You can anticipate what might go wrong and make your choice with those variables in mind. Not doing so ends up in a bad decision.

You've Always Done It That Way

You're pretty sure of yourself. You've made good decisions in the past. What else is new? The answer could be *a lot.* Your industry may have made a dramatic change in a short period of time. You could have lost a key person in your organization who covered for you and your bad decisions. You may be using out-of-date data and assumptions. Simply trusting your gut based on the past won't work here.

You're Too Isolated

Most of us think that our ideas and our worldview is the best, if not the only one, that should prevail. However, in today's world economy, there are many different cultures, beliefs, and philosophies, and they won't all line up with you and your beliefs. It behooves you to get out and talk to people. Participate in other cultures, both work and social. Go to conferences and events where differing ideas are presented. You'll find your intuition is stimulated, and more creative and varied ideas and opportunities will pour forth.

You're Not Talking to Key People

You may have made a good intuitive decision but the people around you need to understand it. Again, most decisions are not purely intuitive. You'll need to back up some of those decisions and its rational implications with actionable items for your team. There's nothing worse than a key player in a company who appears to make decisions on a whim. It leaves a very demoralized workforce.

You Haven't Balanced the Intuitive With Logic

Many people interviewed for this book are gut trusters. They come up with great ideas almost like magic. They quickly know things about people, situations, and future trends that others take a long time to research and investigate. However, almost all of them said they back up their hunches by following through to see if their insight is accurate. Once they have the idea, they call in their experts and test out their theories. Or, if they run a solo or small business, they test with a small sample of clients. That's where you can see if that magic has wings!

You Don't Have a Trusted Group of Advisors

When you're making decisions about your business or any area in your life, you need at least a few trusted folks you can lean on. Ideally, these should be people who "get" you and what you're trying to accomplish in life. They're the ones who won't immediately put down your idea because it's "foolish," "hasn't been done before" or is judged plain "wrong" before you've explained it. You want good people who may be in business or not. They could be part of a networking group, a mastermind group, or a trusted friend or relative who doesn't have an investment in the outcome of your decision beyond your happiness and success. Let your ideas fly with them. See what feels right and what doesn't. Think of them as your "Intuitive Support Committee." Those folks are worth their weight in gold.

You Allow Yourself to Stay in Chaos and Drama

Let's face it: Business is about change and it's often tumultuous. That may be the case, but your best decisions are not made when you or your company are in full-blown drama mode. If you're in this place and trying to make an intuitive decision, step back. This doesn't mean you need to take a week off or something similar. It means to schedule some downtime, stare out the window, daydream, do some deep breathing, or meditate. Whatever works for you is fine. That still, small voice is your guide. It must be listened to, valued, and followed. To find that voice, get out of the chaos. Be still and listen. Then follow the wisdom you receive.

Put Your Intuition to Work Tip
Be honest. Re-read the "Why Do People Make Bad Decisions?" section. Which one describes your chronic weakness in decision-making? The next time you're tempted to wing it with, "My gut says _____," pay close attention. Is your weakness showing?

| Closing |

The important thing is not to stop questioning. Curiosity has its own reason for existing. One cannot help but be in awe when one contemplates the mysteries of eternity, of life, of the marvelous structure of reality. It is enough if one tries merely to comprehend a little of this mystery every day. Never lose a holy curiosity.

—Albert Einstein

There are an infinite number of useful techniques you can use to tap into the wonderful wisdom of your intuition. I've described many in the book. We're all different and have diverse ways of experiencing the gentle prompting of our inner guidance. My hope is that you've found several that will become tried and true for you.

I also hope you'll befriend and nurture your intuition. Treat those random thoughts, gut feelings, instincts, dreams, images, and nudges as if they were gifts from a wise friend. Your intuition—your Inner Compass—always has your best interests at heart and will continuously point you in the direction of success and happiness.

| Index |

| *Index* |

| About the Author |

LYNN A. ROBINSON, MEd, president of Intuitive Consulting, Inc., is an international expert on the topic of intuition. She is a best-selling author and motivational speaker who has helped thousands of clients around the world access the power of their intuition.

She has been featured and quoted in *Woman's Day, Redbook,* the *Boston Globe,* the *Chicago Tribune,* the *New York Times, USA Today,* and many others. She has appeared on *Anderson Cooper,* as well as on ABC and FOX News.

Lynn's seven books have been translated into more than a dozen languages. They include *Divine Intuition: Your Inner Guide to Purpose, Peace and Prosperity* and *LISTEN: Trusting Your Inner Voice in Times of Crisis.*

Lynn has been sought out by celebrities, entrepreneurs, and executives for her intuitive advice and counsel. She advises business owners, CEOs, and other individuals to help them fine-tune their intuition in order to make healthy and successful personal and professional decisions.

We all have an inborn guidance system capable of providing clear and accurate direction to create a successful life. But there are times when we need the "extra" insight that only a gifted intuitive can provide.

A session with Lynn will give you:

    ⊦   Clarity about your vision, plans, and next steps.

    ⊦   Creative marketing ideas for your department, product, service, or company.

ⱶ   Insight about partnerships, peers, employees, or potential hires.

ⱶ   An intuitive sounding board.

ⱶ   Ideas to create more abundance and prosperity.

Whatever the format, Lynn's message is always the same: Too often, people resist the urge to trust their intuition—their Inner Compass. But when we follow its wisdom, we are led to success, happiness, and a greater sense of purpose.

To learn more, go to *www.LynnRobinson.com*.